MY "SECRET LOVE" AFFAIR WITH DORIS DAY

by Michael J. DeVita

DEDICATION

The title probably best indicates to whom this book is being dedicated. Doris Day has been the one constant in my life from the age of 8 till the present time. She has been an idol, a friend, a confidant, a pen pal, a role model, a sister I wish I had had (in addition to the three I already have)…almost anything important to me. Her music has been a daily dose of the best of all vitamins, and I have spent most of my life collecting, listening to and searching for everything she has ever recorded or sung that was never recorded. Her movies have been a constant source of pleasure throughout my life, as has the correspondence between us for over 65 years! Best of all, Doris always makes me smile, an important thing in anyone's life.

I also dedicate this book to all the family and friends who have tolerated my love for Doris all my life. They have been most understanding and very supportive. They always knew that no matter what else, it was always "Love Me/Love Doris!"

In addition, I would like to express my special thanks to three people (all published authors) who gave me suggestions and advice in this venture: Dick Biggs, Paul Brogan and Susan Schoeffield. Without their help and suggestions, the project may never have seen fruition. Susan, especially, was there for me every step along the way, and I truly appreciate it.

PREFACE

While portions of this story are illustrated with details of my personal life and relationships, they are only mentioned in an effort to give background for the broadest scope of this book, that being my long time affinity for Doris Day. So, if some members of my family (as characters in the story) are only briefly mentioned and not fully developed, that is not the purpose of the narrative. They are mentioned only as enablers. You will see why.

In case you wonder why I do not include a section of photos, I would invite you to visit the "Just Doris" pages and the other pages on my website (www.sampod4u.com), where there are many.

IN THE BEGINNING....

I guess all my life has been about music, in some way or another, whether it be listening, watching or singing. I do not have many memories before the age of 5, at the time when my Mother died. I don't recall there being much music played at our home on Cedar Street in Allentown, Pennsylvania, and that was long before the age of television. As a family, we were pretty much into not much. Dad worked half the day and late nights. His chosen occupation was that of a waiter and sometimes bartender. He worked in some pretty fancy places during the course of his life and while he worked at Marconi's Restaurant in the very heart of downtown Baltimore, Maryland, he was the most often requested waiter by "stars" who were returning to town for their performances either at the Lyric or Morris Mechanic Theatre, in the days long before the Hippodrome Theatre decided to reinvent itself with what are probably the most uncomfortable seats in the world.

Mom read, listened to the radio or talked on

the telephone, and my sister and I played games. We listened to the radio, too, and enjoyed programs like "Let's Pretend" or funny man, "Spike Jones." And who could forget being scared by "The Shadow" or the Molle Mystery Theater. In fact, I remember lots of great radio shows. Today, I cannot name nearly as many good TV shows. When Dad was at home for any amount of time, he was usually at his mother's house (half a block away) with his brother Harry. The more happy times in my earliest memory were those I spent other places than at the house with Mom and Dad.

Before I get too much further in this story, you need to understand my use of the words "Mom" and "Mother". I was a lucky guy. In my life, I got to call three women "Mom". One was my birth mother until she died when I was a five year old. Her name was Rose, and my sister was named after her. I hate to say I remember very little about my birth mother, but the facts are the facts. The second "Mom" is my maternal Grandmother Victoria, who raised me after her daughter died until I was 9 years old, then off and on after that. The last but not least of my three moms would be my step-mother Thelma, who became my Mother when Dad remarried. (I never called her step anything.) She was Mom, unless my grandmother Victoria was around. If she was, to circumvent confusion, I called Thelma "Mother." My paternal grandmother was always "Grammy." I never in any way confused her with a term for mom or mother. To me, she was not the mothering type.

That said, "Grammy", my Dad's mother Jenny, lived up the street, and we were often there playing with my cousin Mike (both of us were named for Grammy's husband, the one none of us had ever seen.) Grammy was married long enough to produce four children (four years in a row), and then her husband left her because he did not want to live in such a large family. Grammy and her sisters pitched in, and she managed. She was a tough lady and nothing was going to get her down. I regret the fact that I did not set up a historical record with her while she was still alive. That does not mean I would have learned anything about her husband; she would never discuss him. My father had two brothers and one sister. They are the ones who became my official aunts or uncles on this side of the family: Harry, Mary (his wife), Pete (who was killed in World War II), Lena (the only daughter) and Phil (Lena's husband). I say official because on this side of the family, "aunt" or "uncle" were always used when saying their names. It was, after all, the formal side of the family.

Even my father did not have many memories of his father Michael, but the custom was to name the children after the father, and so Dad and his brother Harry complied. It caused a bit of confusion and some fun gags as well. But we settled on "Big Mike" and "Little Mike". I was the older, so it was my fate to pick up the nickname of Big Mike. Little Mike was about 6 or 8 inches taller. I was always a "shrimp" who never got any taller than 5'4". But *Big Mike* it was, and it would be a much more fitting name today, not that I have gotten any taller, only wider. That reminds me of a song that was very popular when I was growing up, and we used to laugh at it. It is not so funny today. It was called "Mr. Five by Five" (*he's five feet tall and he's five feet wide*).

Little Mike's mother was one of my favorite aunts. Aunt Mary was a lot of fun. She really cared about kids, and it showed. She always had time for us no matter how busy she was. She was a great cook, and she always had something to share. She also made chores a lot of fun. If we came to visit and she was doing dishes or cleaning, we would help and enjoyed doing it. And if she was going somewhere, we were always invited along...and that included trips to the movies. In fact, I remember, years later, when I was visiting Allentown for Christmas at the end of 1954. My mother Thelma and Dad were staying at Grammy's, and *Young at Heart* had just opened. I was dying to see it. Aunt Mary talked my mother into going (Mom loved movies *and* Doris Day). So she, my mom and I went to see the movie in the afternoon. When it was over, they were both crying. Aunt Mary looked at me and said: "would you like to see it again?" She called home and made other arrangements for dinner. We had a quick dinner at a local drug store counter; they were prevalent in those days. Just try to find one today. Then we went back and saw the movie a second time, enjoying it just as much the second time through. I have to admit, I much preferred Gig Young over Frank Sinatra for Doris. I could not understand how the character she played could have picked Frank over Gig. I still can't! I loved the songs she sang in the movie, especially one called "Ready, Willing and Able". I really liked the beach scene with Doris and Gig, and the follow up

5

"Hold Me In Your Arms". And I always loved the hauntingly beautiful song based on a classical piece called "Till My Love Comes To Me". What should have been a Top Ten Hit from the movie ("There's A Rising Moon") was never released as a single…just one of many examples of how poorly Columbia Records handled Doris Day's songs…in fact, her entire recording career. More on that later.

But there I go, getting ahead of the story. Grammy (Dad's Mom) kind of kept to herself, and when Uncle Harry was at home, he spent a lot of his time with her, especially if my Dad was there as well. Funny, I can picture Dad, Uncle Harry and Grammy at the big kitchen table, talking, drinking, playing cards and enjoying each other, but I don't see my Mother or my Aunt in the picture. Uncle Harry worked for Mack Trucks, whose center of operations was in Allentown. When the plant closed, he bought a bar and grill and stayed open for many years. Once that happened, it was Aunt Mary who became queen of the kitchen, with homemade cooking dishes popular all over Allentown. People came in droves to eat her Italian meals for many, many years. She was a much better cook than her mother-in-law but never got that credit from family. Funny thing: wives rarely get credit; mothers do.

Uncle Harry and Aunt Mary had an apartment on the second floor of Grammy's house, and that is where we spent our time visiting. There were also a radio and record player available for us to listen to, and lots of music for dancing. Aunt Mary was a good dancer, and she taught me all she knew. I could do a pretty mean jitterbug at the age of six! And I slow danced pretty well, too. It was my aunts on both sides who had everything to do with my love for music, one of the other constants in my life besides Doris.

Things were totally different at my *other* grandmother's house (my mother's mother) first on Ridge Avenue and later on Emmaus Avenue in Allentown, Pennsylvania. I say that because I have rich memories of a house full of aunts and uncles (mostly 7 or 8 years older than me) who were constantly singing, listening to music, playing games, going to dances and concerts, doing the things kids in their mid and late teens do, and often taking me along. We didn't call them Aunt This or Uncle That because they were more like sisters and brothers, and we were always included in their lives. They didn't think of themselves as aunts or uncles. That is what made it so different. On my father's side of the family, it was always Aunt or Uncle, but not the case on the maternal side of the coin. It is pretty obvious which I liked better.

When my birth mother Rose died, World War II had just begun, and my saddened father enlisted for the duration of the war. (It was one way to deal with his grief.) We were farmed off to our grandmother's house to live with her and all my uncles and aunts. Her name was Victoria, but we called her Mom because everybody else did, and she considered us her children, too. In fact, many times when she called us, she had to run through a litany of names before she got the right one because there were so many. Everyone laughed about that. Mom was a joy in everyone's life, all 4'9" of her. Even as a little kid, I was excited about the fact that I was taller than Mom. We spent many quiet hours together, and I loved those times. I remember a lot of Saturday nights when we would listen to the radio together while she was preparing the humongous Sunday dinners for a family of 25+, who came to eat every week. On Saturday nights, the rest of the family was either working or out on dates. My sister would be spending the weekend at her favorite aunt's place (my father's sister, Aunt Lena). But I cherish all those times I spent with this special grandmother who was so much more than that to me. She was the core of my life, and I loved her very deeply. I think I miss her more than anyone else in my life that is no longer with me, and I am sure she is in a truly special place in heaven.

One of Mom's daughters was named Mickey. I didn't really get to know her at all because she died before my mother did. I do remember, however, very well, her husband Bob Schultz. For all of the years I lived in Allentown, he came to visit Mom at least once a year from where he lived and worked in New York City as a music arranger, especially for Broadway shows. We called him "Uncle Bob", one of the few men on this side of the family who got the formal distinction of being called "uncle". I loved watching and listening to him play the piano for us for hours. We would say, "Can you play.......?" And he would play it. If he didn't know it, he asked us to sing a couple bars, and before a minute was gone, he played that song brilliantly. What a marvelous talent. He has a special place in my early memories because he, too, helped make me appreciate music. He truly missed his Mickey, and I don't think he ever married again. He was a special favorite of my grandmother.

Another of Mom's daughters, Jenny, was one of the older members of the family. By the time I was living in the house, she was married with children and lived on the other side of town. So I only saw her and her family on Sundays for dinner. In later years, she moved next door to Mom, but we still rarely saw her.

While I have fond memories of all my aunts and uncles on this side of the family, and there were many, I mostly think of Buddy, Helen and Anna Marie.

Buddy (real name Dominick) was about 7 years older than me. He treated me like his own brother, and we did lots of things together. I remember when he got his first motorcycle and carried me with him all over town. I was his "little brother", and he was showing me off. He took up for me, too, whenever I got into little fights with the neighborhood bullies. I loved "uncle" Bud; he was an important person to me all my life, the brother most guys want when they don't have one. He worked as a paper boy, and I would go along and help him to deliver papers and collect accounts each month. He also worked at a movie theater as an usher for several years, and I got to see a lot of free movies. Eventually, he became an important accountant for some very big companies. Years later, when he married and had children, I was his baby sitter whenever possible and loved his kids as well. I still do.

Buddy was the cement that held that side of the family together. He was always big on family togetherness, and he was an excellent role model for me about how to become a loving and loyal member of the family. At funerals, weddings, any kind of family get-togethers, if no one else showed up, Buddy was always there to represent the family. He could always be counted on to help, and he never resented giving that help when asked. He died a few years ago, and I miss him all the time. "My Buddy" was very special to me, all my life.

It was Helen and Anna Marie who truly got me interested in music. I was told (by them, and they never lied) that even as a baby, I wanted to be serenaded and rocked to sleep with a special song called "Ti-Pi-Ti-Pi-Tin". Yes, I know...pretty corny... but evidently I loved it. (And apparently I loved it even more when they were the ones who baby sat

11

for me and my sister because they were so much fun.) They were genuine; they really loved us, and it showed. Years later, after Dad had remarried and we were living in Baltimore, whenever he and Mom wanted to go on a vacation and we had to stay home, it was Helen and Anna Marie who came to take care of us, and we loved it! They even enjoyed playing board games with us, and we got along famously. Well, mostly that is. You see, when it came to games, like me, Anna Marie did not like to lose. (Years later, a good game-playing friend of mine really destroyed a game of "Risk" rather than have it available for us to play. She said I just got too competitive.) I should add: in game playing, I still am very competitive. If a game has a winner, then the game is played to be a winner. As my mother used to say, if you don't play to win, why bother?

Helen (for fun, I called her "Aunt Pippy" ...and I honestly cannot remember why) was the eldest living daughter in the family. She was in her 20's and she operated a beauty salon. (Occasionally, she would take us along, and we would run havoc all over the place.) The customers thought we were cute, and we loved the "goodies" they supplied. My sister helped Pippy with the permanents (oh, those stinky permanents), and I helped at the desk, greeting customers, making appointments, answering the phone, and being a little Mr. Business Man. Helen never scolded us for any reason. She was such a loving person that everyone who knew her absolutely adored her. (Not many years later, when I was living in Baltimore, she made sure that I had copies of the latest Doris Day 78-rpm records whenever they came out and got me started on my expensive habit of collecting records). But before that, she was one of those who were instrumental in supporting my admiration of Doris Day. It didn't hurt that she, too, was a fan. I found out that she didn't just buy one copy of a record; she also bought one for herself. (Of course, she reminded me of the fact that as a child I had played many of her records which featured Doris singing with the Les Brown Band, but at the time I was not aware of that. I only know I liked her singing voice.) I know it may sound strange, but even as a little kid, I felt that Doris was singing directly to me. That is something that everyone has said about Doris Day. As a band singer, she was popular worldwide, and most people liked her. Evidently, Helen did, too, or she would not have owned so many of the records with Doris on the vocal. Helen was truly a special lady.

Anna Marie was what one would then have
called a "swinger". She is no longer with us
so she can't hit me for snitching on her.
When she was in her quiet mode (not often),
she would curl up on the sofa, settle down
into a good book (a romance novel, I am
sure), eating either some ripe, black olives
or a combination of pretzel sticks and
chocolate ice cream. She would actually eat
the ice cream by shoveling it in with the
pretzels, something I learned to do, too. The
pretzel and chocolate ice cream combination
was rather tasty. She would gladly share the
ice cream and pretzels, but no one touched
her olives! Anna also loved to dance and
took advantage of every opportunity to do
so, and she had lots of boyfriends who were
on call to take her to local venues. At home,
she would practice new steps with me, and I
loved it, too. Nearby Dorsey Park had a
ballroom, as did places like Lehigh Country
Club and Hershey Park. There was even a
place on a lake that really looked beautiful at
night. We would go along when she got
dropped off and picked up, at first, so I got
to see the places even though we could not
go in. And Anna loved to laugh; she had a
really infectious laugh and got everyone to
join in whenever she found something
funny. She could always brighten up a

dreary mood, and when she wasn't around, I missed her a lot.

As I indicated earlier, both Anna Marie and Helen were directly responsible for my all-encompassing interest in music. They each had a huge collection of 78-rpm records and record players, and I was allowed to play them whenever I wanted. Because of the time period, it was mostly big band recordings with vocal choruses by people who at the time I did not know. (Yes, many were even by Les Brown and his band with vocals by Doris Day). One of my vivid memories of me and the record player was the day Helen married her boyfriend, Tommy. They had the reception in Mom's big back yard. Buddy had set up a record player at a window in the dining room that overlooked the yard. He also had set up the speakers somehow to project out into the crowd. And I got to play all the music. I loved it! I often considered becoming a disc-jockey, but when the time came to make the big decision, I chose college and a career as a teacher of English and Theater for 33 years. I never regretted that choice, and I loved the kids and the job. I even managed to incorporate much music into some of the everyday lessons, and the students seemed to enjoy that a lot. I would never have guessed that one day I would be both a disc jockey and a webmaster in my 70's. It started with deejaying for an internet radio station in 2010, and then running a website, now well into its second year of operation.

All that being said, most of all , I remember the trips to the Steel Pier Marine Ballroom in Atlantic City, New Jersey and one particular evening which was my first real introduction to a great band vocalist named Doris Day. Hearing her on a record was one thing, but seeing her in person was really something quite different, and I remember it vividly to this day.

CHAPTER ONE:

FUN IN ATLANTIC CITY

Before the advent of casinos and fervent gambling and before it got run down, Atlantic City was a very popular place to visit, as far back as the turn of the century. In fact, in the 1890's, it was a plush playground as well as the home of the Miss America Pageant. It had some really ritzy hotels, and the boardwalk was world famous, in person as well as in song. Remember "On the Boardwalk in Atlantic City?" I can offer a couple of links that will give the reader a better idea of what I am about to elaborate. Just type them into the URL bar of your computer.

http://blog.achotelexperts.com/history-of-the-steel-pier/

http://www.victorianamagazine.com/archives/6136

A trip to Atlantic City anytime was great fun but especially in the summer time for a day or even longer. Even as late in my life as when I was in high school in Baltimore, our summer vacations would include two or more weeks visiting Mom and the family in Allentown, and that would often result in at least one trip to Atlantic City for an overnight. When we were kids, Uncle Tommy (Helen's husband/boyfriend) would drive, and in the car would be the two of them, Anna Marie, my sister and I, and sometimes Buddy, if he could get off. Allentown was probably no more than two hours away so it was a nice drive, and we sang all the way. You could smell the salt air even two or three miles away, and when we did, we got all excited and anxious to run and play all day on the huge beaches.

We never had reservations in advance; there were plenty of places to stay on the many side streets off the boardwalk. The grown-ups (Tommy and Helen) would rent a family apartment for the two or three days. I don't know how many it slept, but I remember having my own bed, so it must have been fairly large. We were only there for breakfast and to sleep at night.

Once we settled in, it was a quick walk to the beach. We would spend a pretty good portion of the day on the big beach right next to the Steel Pier. The sand was really soft and white (in most places), the beach was large, and all kinds of vendors marched back and forth selling everything from hot dogs and ice cream and soda to suntan lotion. It was fun jumping the waves. Buddy and Anna Marie were good swimmers, and they swam out beyond the waves. My sister and I were not good swimmers so we stayed close to the beach with Helen and Tommy who kept a watchful eye on us. I got some pretty bad sunburn back then. I do remember being swabbed in suntan lotion, but it did not seem to help. We didn't think about the hurt while we were so busily occupied doing other things.

Buddy tried to teach me to swim, several times, but my reluctance to put my face underwater stifled that effort. One time he actually threw me into the water and said, "Swim!" When he saw that was not going to happen, he quickly dove in to save me. No, I can't swim today either (but that is a whole other story). Another fond memory of that beach in AC was the tar that would get on your feet from standing at the water's edge. Atlantic City, after all, was relatively close to the oil centers of New Jersey.

After an ample amount of time on the beach (always decided by the grown-ups), it was then back to the apartment to clean up, followed by an early dinner and a brief stroll on the boardwalk until we were ready to go to the Pier. The Steel Pier in Atlantic City was one of the most well-known theme parks and attractions world-wide, earning its reputation over the decades for hosting an array of concerts, unusual shows, and the greatest entertainers of the times. It was called *"The Showplace of the Nation!"*

I remember it so vividly because it had three or four movies, some kind of famous entertainer performing on stage, other stage shows (usually kid-oriented), and many attractions like the diving horses who climbed a large platform over the water (horse and rider) and literally dove together into the ocean. There was even a diving bell that took you under water where you were supposed to see all kinds of things. The water was pretty dirty, though, so mostly people saw dirty water and a spare fish or two once in a while. But it was still exciting to be under water without getting wet!

The highlight of the evening (at least for my

aunts) was the hour or two spent at the end of the pier in the enclosed Marine Ballroom, which had an outside deck all around it with ocean views; it was kind of like being on a big ship. To me, it seemed huge and it had windows overlooking the ocean. It was situated on the end of the pier near the diving horses. In the ballroom itself, there was a raised stage on which the bands played, and a big dance floor, for obvious reasons, with chairs along the sides of the walls (not everyone danced). The stage could not have been too high because I remember that I could prop my chin in my hands on the stage and watch up close. Watching a band always fascinated me.

The Marine Ballroom boasted some of the biggest bands of the day, just like the stage show in other parts of the pier featured some of the biggest names of the day. I know that we probably saw The Glenn Miller Band, as well as The Dorsey Brothers, Benny Goodman, and other famous orchestral aggregations. On one special night though, the star band was Les Brown and his Band of Renown featuring Doris Day.

Normally, when we first arrived, we would just jump right in and start to dance to whatever was playing. It didn't matter that my sister Roseanne and I were just kids; it was more like we were at a big wedding reception. Kids danced there, too, and usually with grown-ups leading the way. I loved jitterbugging on the big dance floor with Anna Marie, and sometimes we would have a crowd of 15 or 20 people watching us and egging us on. After one or two dances, though, Anna Marie got claimed by others closer to her age, and we didn't see her again till it was time to go home. I got asked to dance, too, and that felt good to a little boy!

CHAPTER TWO:

ENTER DORIS DAY

As we arrived on this particular night, things were a bit different. Some couples were doing a slow dance on the floor, but most eyes were focused on the stage where, at the microphone, was this tall goddess singing what was one of the top ten songs of the day at the time. It was called "Till The End of Time". I was mesmerized. I had never seen anyone prettier. I had never heard anyone sing anything as beautiful as she sang that song. My feet took me directly to the corner of the stage, where I propped my head in my hands, and I watched and listened and watched some more. I wanted to stay there forever. That lovely lady next sang "Come To Baby Do". This was my first "real" attraction to *any* female, and I was hooked for life. Don't laugh; it's true. Ask any of my friends or family who have had to endure my never-ending Doris Day sermons.

Today, I still give those sermons, especially if I ever hear anyone say they don't know who Doris is. Good Lord!!!

But that night, when Anna Marie asked me to dance, I would not budge. Helen asked me to dance; I still would not budge. So they figured I wasn't going anywhere, and that is where I remained for the better part of 90 minutes. I am not sure of times, but I am guessing we arrived around 8:15 or so. When she was not singing, Doris sat on a chair on the corner of the stage; it just so happened to be the same corner on which I was propped. I am certain she saw me staring throughout the evening when she was not performing because every so often she would look my way and smile…that wonderful smile she still has today. The band would play one or two songs. Then she would sing one or two songs. Then the band came back again. They would take a quick break after 30 minutes or so and start again. (Just so you don't think that I was completely on my own, I felt Helen's eyes on me the whole time. I always knew why she was my mother's favorite sister.) Aged memory does not allow me to recall any more of the songs which Doris sang that evening, but I am sure she sang two of the band's biggest hits, "Sentimental Journey" and "My Dreams Are Getting Better All The Time" at some point while we were there.

It is hard for me to explain how this event became probably the most emphatic one of my life, but it surely was. Physically, I got goose bumps when I heard Doris sing… something that rarely happens to me now unless I truly hear a marvelous voice. With Doris, I got them every time. From that point on, it was always Doris Day first, second and third, and everyone else after that. I had lots of favorite male singers; no female singers were rivals for Doris. I liked some others okay, but no one else was close…not ever.

When ten o'clock rolled around that evening, it was time to leave. (Not for the band; I am sure they played on till about 11 or 12, but we kids belonged in bed.) At least Helen and Tommy thought so. But when they told me it was time to go, I wasn't going anywhere. They asked me several times; they even threatened (useless…it didn't work). And then Helen got a brainstorm.

As Doris finished another set of songs and sat in her chair, Helen waved Doris to the corner of the stage and asked if she would help convince me that it was time to go home. Doris tried, but I did not want to go. I wanted to stay and hear her sing more. Then we made a deal. She promised that she would keep in touch and would correspond with me if I would write to her, which sounded like a good plan. She gave an address to Helen. She then promised to autograph my hand, which she did in blue ink. (I thought I would never wash it again). She also gave me a signed copy (signed on the 78-rpm label) of "Sentimental Journey". It is the first of many treasures that I still have in my Doris Day collection.

That night I did not want to wash my hand, nor the next morning, but after a day or two, of course, the signature wore off. But the moment never has. We have corresponded off and on ever since that first night. I wonder if Doris remembers that night and the little boy who could not take his eyes off of her. She remembers me, but that is because I don't let her forget, and this past year, she honored me with a place on her webpage that refers to me as her "friend", and she sent a verbal message which you can listen to on the www.sampod4u.com website. Thus, that is how the "affair" began. It continues to the present day.

CHAPTER THREE:

WHERE IS DORIS?

Of course, my first big task after that "Marine Ballroom Encounter" was to try to contact Doris by mail. Believe me, I tried and tried for weeks and weeks but to no avail. She had given Helen an address, but when Helen went to look for it in her purse, it wasn't there. She was so apologetic, but as I said earlier, no one could ever not like Helen. We tried everything we could collectively think of to locate her. Obviously, at that time, she was traveling with the Les Brown Band and constantly on the road so reaching her by letter would have been pretty difficult with or without an address. I hate to say it took almost three and a half years to make contact, but I don't give up easily. And best of all, when it finally happened, Doris remembered me!

Meanwhile, I was busily learning all I could about my new found love. When we got back to Allentown, I did a diligent search through all the records in the house (Anna's and Helen's and even Aunt Mary's collection at my other grandmother's house). There were hundreds and hundreds of 78 rpms by dance bands, and a lot of them were on Okeh and Columbia labels, which are the labels on which Les Brown recorded. (At the time, Okeh was a subsidiary of Columbia). At any rate, I managed to find twenty-four records by Les Brown and His Band (with vocal chorus by Doris Day). My expert begging and cajoling allowed these to become part of my record collection, joining that special signed copy of "Sentimental Journey". That went along with my very first record player that Helen gave me for my birthday as an additional apology for losing the address. Just one more reason to love Aunt Pippy more and more! And I played those records. I played them and played them and played them again. (I have to admit that the other members of the household were very indulgent of my excesses.) Some of those early recordings are among my Doris favorites, even today. Off the top of my head, I can quickly pick out: "Long Ago and Far Away", "Ah Yes, There's Good Blues Tonight", "My Number

One Dream Came True" and "Sooner or Later". Do I still have them? Absolutely. I would not part with them for anything, nor do I let anyone else touch them since they are such collector's items and they are not replaceable.

One night, Tommy came home from work, grabbed me and pushed me into the car. I had no idea where we were rushing off to, but it was about 10 blocks away to a local bar. (Other than the bars which my Uncle Harry owned or my Aunt Lena and Uncle Phil owned in Pennsylvania, I had never been in a bar per se.) As I discovered, this visit had nothing to do with the bar but everything to do with a piece of equipment on display within. I was accustomed to jukeboxes; I always had nickels ready, whenever we found one, to play some of my favorite Doris Day records which were always on the jukeboxes, but I had never before seen a *panoram* and had never heard of "soundies". This was like a big square TV screen, and it sat on top of the bar counter. Remember, this was a good 8 or 10 years before TV ever become so well known. Anyway, Tommy sat me on a bar stool, put what I think was a quarter in the machine (very expensive compared to the nickel machines), and he clicked on one soundie called *My Lost Horizon*. And there on the screen came The Les Brown Band featuring Doris Day singing that song. It was the earliest example of MTV. I was in heaven...there she was again, not in person, but I could still see her sing, and I adored it. I cannot remember the number of times I walked those 10 blocks to listen again or to ask Mr. Pat (the bartender) if there were any new ones. I believe Doris made 3 or 4 of these, but this is the only one I remember seeing as a little kid. With the twenty plus records and occasional visits to the soundies, I was doing well in the Doris Day department, except for actual contact. You have to admit I certainly had a lot of allies in my Quest For Doris and this on-going "affair".

CHAPTER FOUR:

1945 AND ITS AFTERMATH

My Dad, who was stationed in Germany, was a diligent letter-writer. In that respect, he is much like Doris. Even today, if you write to her, it will take a while, but she always responds. Mom had to give me a big shove to get me to respond to Daddy's letters, but I did...even then I was told I had terrible handwriting (the only subject in school in which I did not do well.) Nick was an excellent father regardless of how far away he was. It didn't matter; he even corresponded with my teachers. I remember them telling me that they had received a letter from him checking up on me. Dad had, of course, heard all the news, and I was constantly teased about my "affair" with Doris. He was doing that in good fun because years later, I would tease him about his thing for Connie Francis, definitely *not* my taste. Dad loved singers when they occasionally threw in a little Italian, like Connie did. Yes, he liked Dean Martin, too. I tried to point out to him years later that Doris did the Latin thing with "Que Sera, Sera", but he would not bite. Unfortunately, he did not live long enough to hear her *Latin for Lovers* album; he would have loved it.

In the summer of 1945 something very special happened. World War II ended, and my dad came home. Of course, his first stop was Allentown to visit us. After a few hours with the family, he took us to my other grandmother's house for some time with them. We thought he was going to be with us all the time. That was good news, but if it meant leaving Mom and Helen and Anna and Buddy and the rest...that was not good news at all. Things were up in the air, but not for too long. Dad's brother, Pete, who had been killed in the war, still had a big bedroom in the old house. It was now vacant, and Grammy talked Daddy into moving there. That meant he could see us often (less than 10 miles from one house to the other), and we could stay where we were. Hooray!)

Dad has always worked in the area of food and wine. In Germany, he was a company cook. So, he took a job not too far away from Grammy's house as Manager of the Lehigh Country Club. We saw him when he was not working, and he spent a lot of his off-time with his brother Harry and sister Lena, who owned a bar in Freemansburg, Pennsylvania. We often joined him when he visited Aunt Lena because she had lots of kids our age, and we had a big place to play in (not the bar room). Before long and no longer grief stricken, Dad met Thelma, who came from Houston, Texas, complete with a Southern drawl and appropriate charm. She was a real sweetie. I loved her, too. I especially loved her accent and teased her whenever she said "Y'all".

She was currently living with her daughter, Dolores, and working in Bethlehem. She had left her second husband and somehow migrated to the ABE area of Pennsylvania, otherwise known as Allentown-Bethlehem-Easton area. When she arrived there in Pennsylvania, she fell in love with the mountains and decided to stay. She and Dolores shared an apartment near my Uncle Phil and Aunt Lena's bar, and they used to come in after work for dinner and a drink. Thelma was introduced to my Dad by my Uncle Phil, who thought they would make a good match...he was certainly right. I don't think the thought of marrying again anytime soon was on my father's mind, even though members of the family on both sides were working hard on what they conceived to be a big problem...a dad with two kids who really needed a mother. We didn't know we needed one...we had a mom. But the grownups thought otherwise.

We liked Thelma and Dolores right away. I called Thelma "Honey" and told her I wanted to marry her. Talk about falling in love! Big problem. Daddy was in love with her, too, and we had no idea they were planning to tie the knot. I called Dolores "Sis" because that is what "honey" called her. Little did I know she would soon be my step-sister. I really do dislike that term "step". It doesn't explain anything about relationships at all. She would be my sister through marriage. That is enough explanation. She wasn't step anything; in fact, we really enjoyed each other's company; we still do. Dolores is a lovely lady, and she reminds me of Doris. Funny thing about that. Over the years, Sis has been stopped several times on the street-people asking her for autographs, confusing her with Doris. She was always honest and never faked one, but now you know only one of the reasons why she is one of my favorite people. The fact that we spent hours together playing Doris records is another. We really liked each other and Doris.

At any rate, Roseanne and I got along famously with both of them. They took us on outings to Hershey and Dorney Parks, two amusement parks that were very popular at the time. (They have become very big parks today; at that time, they were just popular fun places to visit.) We did all kinds of things together; I guess we did not realize it at the time, but it was a way of getting us all together and a start on putting the family back together again. Dad had us (my sister Roseanne and me); Thelma had Dolores (and two sons, Bruce and Dale, back in Texas living with their father, her first husband). If we ever all did get together in the same house, that would be a fairly large family of eight. That only happened very rarely and usually at Christmas time. Texas was a far cry away, and we did not always have the money to send for Bruce and Dale so I really never felt the camaraderie.

To top things off (at least for me), both Honey and Sis were Doris fans, too. Honey used to play "My Dreams Are Getting Better All The Time" a lot. I guess the song reflected what was happening in her own life. Many a day, down the road a few years,

the three of us would put on a Doris record
and listen to it together. I especially
remember one special one. All three of us
liked it for different reasons, and all three of
us came home with it one day (each with a
separate single), and we wore all three of
them down to the cardboard beneath the
wax. That song was: "(Where Are You)
Now That I Need You" from the Betty
Hutton movie, *Red, Hot and Blue*. Betty
sang the song ok and she also sang it in the
movie, but no one sang it like Doris. Today,
it is on my list of my Top Favorite 50 Doris
Day Records. No...I can't just pick 10 or
20...50 would be the very least. Out of
almost a thousand songs that Doris sang, 50
does not seem like too big a favorites list,
does it? Or even a hundred for that
matter…but never less than 50.

CHAPTER FIVE:

DISAPPEARING ACTS

Kind of suddenly, sometime in 1946, things I did not much like began to happen in various places in both my world and the world at large. The Big Bands started to disappear. Once in a while, Mom and I would hear Doris and Les on the radio if there was a Big Band Broadcast, usually on a Friday night. But, in no time at all, these broadcasts diminished, and the bands did as well. Recently, someone asked the question "why did big bands die out?" on the website, www.answers.com . This was their very excellent response:

" As with any musical style, peoples' tastes changed over time. However, there were a number of factors specific to the big bands that caused their demise as the most popular form of music.

First, the price of attendance at dances and concerts in the 1930s/40s was artificially low. Theaters would feature both a band and a film, with the film in effect subsidizing the band's appearance. Also the recording companies had a lot of power and held down salaries - many musicians were paid straight wages rather than a percentage of a recording's gross or net profit, no matter how many copies were sold. By keeping costs low, it was possible for most venues to feature as many as 15 or 20 musicians at a time. But as the bands gained popularity, many of the musicians started to demand a piece of that success. This resulted in two strikes.

The first strike was in 1941 against ASCAP, the American Society of Composers, Artists, and Publishers. Orchestras were allowed to keep performing and recording but only if they didn't feature ASCAP songs. To compensate, arrangers looked for any and every tune they could find that was in the public domain. There were swing versions of melodies by Ravel and Tchaikovsky, even kids' songs such as "Where O Where Has My Little Dog Gone?"" Solos had to be written out instead of improvised, just to ensure that a musician didn't accidentally slip in a bar or two from an ASCAP song.

While there was still a lot of good music performed, overall quality fell because of those restrictions.

The second strike was much more serious in its length and damage. Despite the first strike, musicians were still pretty much under the thumb of the recording companies. So in July 1942 the musician's union imposed a ban on all recording. Live performances were still allowed but no records could be made. This couldn't have come at a worse time because most bands were facing wartime travel restrictions and couldn't perform new songs in person in nearly as many places. Recordings would have been an important way of keeping their music before the general public. The recording companies exploited a loophole in the ban that allowed singers to continue to make records. They put together vocal groups who sang what would have been the instrumental parts of a song a cappella, and fronted them with some of the popular singers of the time such as Dick Haymes and Frank Sinatra. It was contrived and not very good, but it had the effect of keeping the singers in the public eye, while instrumental musicians were limited to whatever public performances they were able to make. When musicians' unions finally negotiated settlements with each record company, they quickly found that their popularity had been eclipsed by the singers. The strike settlement also brought with it much higher salaries, but doing so priced them out of the market for ballrooms and theaters. Fans weren't willing or able to spend several times what they had before the war to see the same performances.

The war itself also affected the bands in several ways. A number of the most popular leaders such as Artie Shaw, Larry Clinton, Claude Thornhill, and Glenn Miller had gone into the armed forces so they were no longer leading their bands in public. Among the bands that continued, so many musicians were drafted that some sections would go through a complete rotation of personnel in less than a month. Retirees and high-school band members were being recruited, resulting in lower performance quality in many cases. Then there was the sheer fact that a huge number of potential fans were working for Uncle Sam. While they listened to a lot of recorded music, they were in no position to go to a Saturday dance. After the war ended these potential fans were occupied with recovering as much as four years of their lives that had been put on hold. They had to concentrate more on

*returning to school, starting a family, and
finding a job as opposed to going to dances.*

*Finally, a number of music critics have
contended that had Glenn Miller lived, just
the force of his creativity and musical sense
might have slowed the bands' decline. It's
difficult for us to realize just how large a
part of the music scene he was - his
popularity by several measures exceeded
that of both Elvis Presley and The Beatles,
so his loss was not just that of one among
many musicians but went to the core of
popular jazz. About the only possible
analogy would be to imagine the state of
rock music had The Beatles been killed in a
plane crash in 1966, or had Elvis died in
1954."*

To compound matters, at least in my world,
Doris Day had left the Les Brown Band. She
had gone to get married, for the second time.
I didn't know it at the time, but she had
already been married and divorced once and
had a son who often accompanied her on the
road. So I lost track of her for another year.
No more records were released that year; no
more soundies. Doris was gone, and I felt
forlorn.

And gone also were my Dad and my Honey.

Dad had an offer from the owner of The
Stafford Hotel in Baltimore, Maryland
to come to Baltimore as Maître d' hotel and
Thelma was offered the job as cashier. At
the time, it was a fairly classy place, and
they jumped at the offer. They told us they
were going to accept the jobs and start
looking for places for us to come and join
them and start a new family. Before 1946
was out, they had gotten married in a small
ceremony at a church across from the
Stafford Hotel. Honey was now my step-
mother, a name that still has far too many
negative connotations. In her honor, I never
called her that horrible name and only
referred to her as "Mother". And we were
always her children...all of us! (I didn't
really start calling her "mom" until after my
grandmother had died years later). "Mother"
always seemed too formal, but she always
understood. I think she was just glad that we
loved her enough to call her that.

Dolores remained in Allentown. Buddy's
older brother, Pat, had also returned from
the war. It was a grand reunion. Two years
earlier, the family had received a telegram
saying he was "lost in action". I remember
vividly the night that telegram arrived; there
were tears shed everywhere. I was too young
to understand what all that meant. I just was

told he was never coming back. But home he came, and it was a surprise for everyone. I am not sure how or when it happened; I just know that somehow he met "sis", and they became inseparable. Mom did not approve, but then as a good, old-fashioned Italian lady, she didn't approve of Dad and Thelma either. Thelma had been twice divorced, and Mom did not approve of divorce. Dolores was the child of a divorced woman, so she did not want Dolores as a potential partner for her son. She regretted that later. Anyway, Dolores and Pat, at least for a while, became an item, and he filled in for my missing Dad. Pat and Dolores then entered our world on a regular basis, and we loved it. And ... you guessed it ... Pat loved Doris Day, too. He said all the soldiers overseas were in love with her because of the success of "Sentimental Journey". It was a perfect anthem for the end of the war years. Besides, Doris was really good looking, and armed servicemen loved good looking women of any age. Dolores was really good looking, too!

CHAPTER SIX:

MOM, COME HERE ... IT'S DORIS!

On Saturday nights, there was a special routine in Mom's house in Allentown early in 1947. Tommy and Helen were married and lived about 6 blocks away. Jenny, another daughter, was married and lived in a house not too far. Anna Marie worked for the telephone company, and she always worked late on Saturday nights. Buddy was working three jobs so he was rarely at home (that was compounded by the fact that he was dating a girl he had met that year, Reba, who eventually became his wife). Pat was usually out with Dolores until Mom put a kabosh on that.

And Mom? She was working on Sunday's dinner. Mom was always working on something; I don't recall her ever resting very much. It was an all-out effort most of

45

the day on Saturday and that night, as she made her special spaghetti sauce from scratch, and prepared all the meats, etc. As I indicated earlier, Sunday's at Mom's house were always a super feast that was really extraordinaire. But as she did all the preparations on Saturdays, she would sip her stronger than Starbuck's coffee, and we had the radio tuned to NBC. When she wasn't actively working on the dinner, we would play 500 Rummy. And I anxiously waited to hear the Top Tunes of the day on *Your Hit Parade*. Frank Sinatra had been the guest host of late, and I sort of liked him. But I liked him better when he introduced his co-host for the new season, Doris Day!!! I was in my glory.

Mom had slipped into the kitchen for something when I heard that special announcement. I yelled, "Mom...Come here! It's Doris!" She came running (only because I had yelled and she thought there was something wrong). Once she found out what it was, she slipped into the dining room, picked up the telephone and called Helen (after all, Helen was a Doris fan, too!) I was beside myself. Doris...on the radio... every week...with Frank Sinatra. And now, I knew where to write:

Miss Doris Day
c/o NBC Radio

And so I wrote. And so she got the letter.
And so she responded. And so I was in 7th
Heaven! She said:

"Dear Michael

*How nice of you to get in touch with me
after all this time. I am so sorry that we
lost contact but let's stay in touch now.
What a sweet letter from you; I will
treasure it. I do remember well the
little boy staring at me all night on the
bandstand. Keep listening, and I will
keep singing.*

*Fondly,
Doris Day"*

That was our very first correspondence,
which continued year after year and
continues to the present day. I have
scrapbooks filled with letters and lots of
autographed pictures from Doris. I call it
my true treasure trove.

The *Hit Parade* show usually went off at 9

p.m. At 9:15 Helen called, and we discussed our mutual happiness at Doris' return to the limelight. In no time at all, we began to hear her as guest star on other radio shows if we caught them on time. In one letter, Doris indicated that she had signed her first recording contract as a single act with Columbia Records. I couldn't wait to continue building my record collection.

Frank always used to introduce Doris when she sang a song on *Your Hit Parade*. He always had such wonderful things to say about her. Years later, he said she was like "a convention of angels". What a truly lovely sentiment. And Doris always had nice things to say about Frank, too. Most of the family especially liked it when Doris sang up- tunes like "Feudin' and Fightin' " or a lively polka. Even Mom's husband (Matthew, or "Pop") liked it when she sang a polka. Like my Dad, he wouldn't admit he liked Doris, too!

I just realized I haven't said much about Pop. He was a nice guy and always trying to improve his mind (and mine). He had stacks of magazines, and he was always referring me to articles I should read. I wish I could recall the names of some of the magazines; I am pretty sure they would be rarities today, but most were of the nature of *National Geographic*, full of pictures and lots of interesting information.

Like his wife, Pop was a hard worker. He worked for the city of Allentown as a maintenance man. Before that, when we lived on Ridge Avenue, he used to be an independent jeweler. He had a vast collection of jewelry, and the front room of the house was a storefront with a jewelry store. There was a door towards the back wall which led into the rest of the house where the family lived. I honestly do not remember many customers or much traffic into the jewelry store, but kids at that age seldom notice things of that sort. I know it was a house with four floors and big rooms, and we always had a good time both inside and out of doors.

Pop also had a truck with built-in display units, and he used to travel to the little towns in and around Allentown with his truck and displays and sell the jewelry. (He took me along on a lot of the trips, and I always had a good time.) Today, that really seems strange, but back then, it really wasn't. And when Pop came in to the little towns, he was very popular and often invited into various homes (with me intact) for coffee and dessert.

When it was no longer profitable to keep the jewelry business open, he sold the business and the house and moved to Emmaus Avenue and had a small farm. He worked for the city by day, and when he got home, he worked some more on the farm. He grew all kinds of vegetables. My sister and I used to pick the bugs off the plants, and Pop gave us pennies for helping. It was an early lesson for both of us in doing work to make money. Pop also raised rabbits, and had grape vines from which he made homemade wine. (awful stuff and we all had to drink a small glass with each dinner meal). It was supposedly good for us. I am not sure how so. I still remember the female members of the family squealing with delight after the jewelry store closed, and he gave all of them little trinkets (like cameos). Everyone liked Pop, too.

Once we had heard that Doris signed a contract with Columbia Records, we could not wait to find the single records. Helen came home one night with several 78-rpm records, the first ones recorded by Doris on Columbia. We listened to them all night long. My special favorite was called "My Young and Foolish Heart". Doris was finally taking off on her own, and I couldn't have been happier for her and for me. It was November of that year when Frank introduced Doris on the Hit Parade show to sing her new hit record, "Papa, Won't You Dance With Me". We loved it. The whole country did, too…And Doris was off and running. HOORAY! Before May rolled around in 1948, she had a number one record on the *Hit Parade*, a million-seller with Buddy Clark as her duet partner on a two-sided hit, "Love Somebody" and "Confess". It was on the radio almost every time I turned it on, and that made me smile. "You go, girl..."

"The right place at the right time" is an adage that fit Doris very well for much of her recording career, and I guess her movie career, too. She was with Les Brown, after leaving twice for marriages that did not work out, at the end of 1945 when "Sentimental Journey" became the #1 record of the year, and "My Dreams Are Getting Better All The Time" was also one of the Top Ten Tunes of the year. She was singing at a party when she was asked to do an audition for the lead part in *Romance on the High Seas*, a role originally offered to Betty Hutton, which she had turned down. So Doris became a leading lady in her first film.

51

She was on *Your Hit Parade* and *The Bob Hope Show*, both of which became big showcases for her songs, especially songs like "It's Magic", which became another massive #1 hit on the Hit Parade. Being in the right place brought her many great opportunities. And that is a good thing for her legions of fans. It made me very happy, too.

CHAPTER SEVEN:

A MOVE FOR ME

It took two years for Thelma and Dad to set up a home in Baltimore. We were not complaining because the final settlement would mean leaving our happy home with Mom and Pop and family and starting all over again in a new place. But in short order we were transported to Baltimore, Maryland and a house in downtown Baltimore which had three floors. We were told it was a temporary arrangement while a brand new home was being built in the Towson Area of Baltimore County. And so we settled in, but I was really homesick for Allentown. That caused a lot of problems. More on that later.

Our Baltimore City house was on Harford Road. It was a fun house in which to live The front door opened into a living room and master bedroom. That led into a hallway (and another exterior door, which entered the house from an alleyway that led from the front street on Harford Road to the back street on Lanvale Avenue). The hallway then led into a large dining room, a small kitchen and a bath. There was also a nice back porch. Where the entranceway came in to the side of the house was a stairwell to the 2nd floor where there was an apartment (which Dad rented out). The stairs also led up to a third floor with a walk-out window on the roof. Many a night, we would sit on that back roof and just enjoy the cool evening from on high. At the top of the stairs was a large bathroom. The hallway led into two bedrooms. My sister Roseanne and I occupied the first bedroom and Dolores was in the front bedroom, which she shared with Baby Sandy. Dolores became both a strong member of the family and a built-in baby sitter, while Mother and Dad continued to work.

As for my Uncle Pat (Dolores' sometimes boyfriend), he honored Mom's edict not to marry the child of a divorce. He married a young Allentown girl named Helen. They married quickly and had two children in short order. After very few years, Pat was stricken with a heart attack and died. If Mom had not liked Dolores, she liked Helen less. Pat was her first born, and nobody was good enough for him. (I personally think that had he married Dolores, they would still be enjoying life together.) Dolores was/is a delightful person; they would have been a great match. Such is life. In fact, all three of my sisters are delightful people and are very much loved. I could not ask for any better.

I neglected to mention that there was also a window on the third floor in the back bedroom of the house overlooking the alleyway. A lot of people (mostly kids) used to cut through the alley as a shortcut from Harford Road to Lanvale. My sister and I learned how much fun it could be to drop bags filled with water on their heads to deter the short routes! Does it sound familiar? Like something you may have seen in a Doris Day movie? Remember the water balloons in *Please Don't Eat The Daisies*? We definitely could identify with those scenes.

There were several other plus factors at the new house. One was the fact that it was two doors away from the corner drug store, which also had a lunch counter, and a soda fountain (wonderful cherry cokes) and a big jukebox. The owner had it loaded with Doris Day records, and that made Sis and me very happy. If we were not listening to Doris on the jukebox, we were playing her records on the record player in Dolores' bedroom and letting Doris lullaby baby sister Sandy to sleep. I don't think Sandy remembers that.

Doris was not the only person we listened to...Dolores had a collection by other artists like Sinatra, Como, Eddy Howard (her favorite), Peggy Lee and Dinah Shore. I still remember us singing along to "Golden Earrings" and "Shoo Fly Pie". (Not to mention all the great songs that Doris put out in those years before her first movie.) Sis really liked "Thoughtless", which Doris sang with The Modernaires and "That's The Way He Does It" and the big hit, "Again".

Another plus factor was that we lived only three short blocks from a neighborhood movie theatre. Saturdays were movie days. If we did all our appointed jobs (Dad was pretty strict about that), then we got our weekly allowance (twenty five cents!) Dad also taught us a great lesson about working for money. We did not just GET and allowance; we worked for one. Dad would make a big chart for the kitchen door, which had all kinds of jobs on it that required attention for the week (everything from taking out the trash, to washing dishes). Each job, upon completion, paid a particular fee (taking out the trash was one cent an occurrence). As we did the jobs, we signed the chart. He would settle with us at the end of the week. It usually worked out to a quarter, which was a big deal back then.

A quarter would take us to the movies and buy us lots of goodies to eat, and we spent almost the entire day (until supper time) watching and re-watching movies and serials all day long. (When we came home, we still had money left for other goodies, like penny candy in the store around the corner.) On special occasions, when Dad was feeling good, he would take Roseanne and me downtown to the first-run theaters on a Sunday for a day at the movies. When that happened we would see one, two and sometimes three movies. It was great. Those days were times for Mother to catch up with Sis and Sandy. I never understood why, but note that I did not include sister Roseanne in that group; she was always "Daddy's Little Girl" until the day he died. Given an option, Roseanne always chose to remain with Daddy before anyone else.

Still another plus in this house was that we were about ten blocks from a big Sear's Department Store. It wasn't the store as much as the gigantic park behind it where we used to play a lot. It had a big hill, and we could lie on the ground and roll all the way down to the bottom. Kids then did not need all the toys and games or electronic gadgets so prevalent in current times. We manufactured our own fun and invented games to play. It would be an understatement to say it was certainly a more innocent time for all concerned.

Some would say that living directly across the street from the local elementary school was also a plus, but we went to a Catholic school about three blocks away that first year. Then, because we would eventually be going to public school after we moved and because of the expense, we wound up in the school across the street for 6th grade. (Going to the Catholic school had made me a close friend to Sister Mary Joseph, and we used to go visit her at the convent next to the school. She was always friendly...and she liked Doris Day, too!!) It seemed like everybody did. (big smile)

My homesickness for Allentown became somewhat of a problem for Mother and Dad. We had to take trips to Allentown for a weekend at least once a month and sometimes more often, and I wanted to spend all my lengthier days off from school in Allentown. The problem was really intensified once we started going to public school; I hated it. I am afraid I became a real pain about that...so much so that Mother and Dad actually let me finish out Elementary School back in Allentown. So I moved back with Mom and the family in Allentown until the beginning of 7th Grade.

This homesick problem lasted well into the early 50's until I graduated from high school. The only time this did not cause a headache for my parents was when Helen, Anna Marie and Buddy came to visit us. And they did on that special occasion when we all went together to see Doris Day for the first time on the big screen.

CHAPTER EIGHT:

A MOVE FOR DORIS

For 7th Grade, we had settled in the brand new house in Baltimore County, and I was getting ready to attend Junior High School Correspondence from Doris had let me know that she was soon starring in a film about romance on a ship. She had left New York and was now at Warner Brothers Studio in California making her first picture. She said that she had actually expected to be traveling on a boat, but that was not the case as the entire film was done on the set. I know she was disappointed because she told me that. She also said she did not realize how naïve she had been.

What a wonderful way to get the summer started back in Baltimore. My favorite aunts and uncle coming to visit and Doris was appearing on the big screen. What could be better than that? (Well...maybe a visit from

Doris!) The big day came, and we all went to see *Romance on the High Seas* together at one of the big first-run theaters in downtown Baltimore.

And I fell in love with Doris all over again. Wow! She was gorgeous, and her voice sounded better and better and better. The big song from the movie, "It's Magic", was nominated for an Academy Award. It lost to some stupid thing called "Buttons and Bows". I have never understood that one. I guess the experts didn't either. Doris was even at the Oscar Ceremonies to sing the song, and everyone thought it would win. What a big disappointment, but not the film. It was hugely popular not only in the US but in the UK, too. Pippy said I had an adoring smile on my face through every minute of the entire movie. Buddy, who was usually non-committal about Doris, said he loved the movie, too. The whole world loved the movie. (It was just the beginning.)

And the hit song was so popular that they renamed the film "It's Magic" in the UK. I was so proud of her; she was a huge success overnight. And that big song topped the *Hit Parade* for over 17 weeks. Once in a while, Doris got to sing it, but since the show was officially Frank Sinatra's, he sang it more, and that made me angry. The policy was that the major star sang the #1 song in each week's broadcast...but the song really belonged to Doris! I got over it. Doris didn't have to. She was so popular by then that she was appearing all over the radio dial on big shows like *The Bob Hope Show*, *The Al Jolson Show*, *Guest Star*, and many others. She was quickly becoming the most talked about and pursued female star in all of Hollywood!

She also must have been getting tons of mail because her correspondence was now often quick and mostly a short picture postcard which she autographed. Funny...sometimes I would get exactly the same picture two or three times in a row; only the message had changed. It took about two years before we started writing actual letters back and forth again. And it was about that time that my aunts convinced me to start arranging everything into scrapbooks. Yes, I still have them, and many of the pages have yellowed and browned. I have to be very careful when I look at the early ones these days because they tend to flake and fall apart, and the rugs are covered with little bits of brown paper My friend, the sampod4u forum moderator Carol in Georgia, says she is going to redo them for me to make them more secure; I look forward to that. I was afraid to mail them in case they should get lost, but with priority mailing these days it should not be a problem.

A quick side note here. As I am writing these words in mid-September of 2011, Doris has just released a new album in the UK called *My Heart*, which contains previously unreleased material that she recorded for her cable TV show *Best Friends* in 1986. The album producers re-mastered the original sessions and added some great hyped up background material. The amazing thing about this is the fact that when it was announced as a pre-order item on Amazon UK, the sales starting hopping very quickly -- so much so that by the time of its actual release on 9/5, it was #1 best seller in vocal/traditional and #3 overall in Pop. It is the first time Doris has had a Top Ten Hit Album in the UK Charts. That in itself would be amazing enough, but seven of her other compilations (including *The Doris Day Christmas Album*) were also riding the UK Charts. At 87, Doris showed that she still has what it takes, and I bet a lot of younger Brits are experiencing this fabulous singer for the first time and liking what they hear. For years, and even today, people forgot that Doris started as a singer;

they remember her as a movie actress. Certainly, their loss….and all those years of catching up on some of the best music ever recorded by anyone!

CHAPTER NINE:

AN ADJUSTMENT
FOR BOTH OF US

So 1948 was a big year for both Doris and me. I moved back to Baltimore and a new phase of my life, junior high school; Doris moved to Hollywood and began a career which would eventually make her the All-Time Female Box Office Queen! She never did realize how exceptionally talented she was. It was a job; she did it and enjoyed it. Even in some of her most recent interviews, she has often commented: "If I could do it, anybody could". Nothing is further from the truth.

Very few people are given the God-granted talents of Doris Mary Ann Kappelhoff, her real name. Few if any other artists have mastered as many different fields as she has in her long career: dancer, band singer, recording artist, lounge singer, movie star, TV star, author, animal activist, hotel owner.

And I guess we should throw in, for good measure, mother and 4x wife (she always said she was better at picking out animals than she was husbands!).

At any rate, 1948 gave Doris some new vistas to conquer; it didn't take her long. She was getting used to a life in Hollywood and juggling the many calls for her appearances (radio shows, concert venues, magazine and newspaper interviews, photo shoots, in person publicity appearances.) She always seemed to enjoy what she was doing. This is evident in her many interviews at the time in hundreds of magazine and news articles and especially in her letters.

No sooner had she made her first movie, which was an overnight smash, then she was pushed immediately into another. Between 1948 and 1968 she appeared in 39 films (an average of two a year). Today, it is an amazing feat if major stars appear in one a year or even every other year. By the end of 1948, she had 7 charted recording hits, and her duets with Buddy Clark were all over the jukeboxes and on the radio as well.

Their first pairing was a two-sided smash and a million-seller. The "A" side was called "Love Somebody" and the flip was

"Confess". This was just a beginning for this popular duo. Before the end of the year, another duet ("My Darling, My Darling") also topped the charts. That just got them set up for the following year and several more chart hits. You could tell from their records how much they enjoyed performing together and how beautifully they got along...but then Buddy was killed in a plane crash and the duets ended for a while, but that is another story. In the years that I have followed her career and read all the interviews and magazine stories, I don't recall her ever reminiscing about Buddy. I am sure she has fond memories of him. After all, they shared her first million-selling gold record. And he called her by that affectionate term, "Dodo", only used by family and close friends. One of these days, I will remember to ask her about her Buddy, especially since I had one of my own.

Side note, 3/1/2012: I had the opportunity via phone to ask Doris about Buddy. She said lots of nice things about him, one being how much of a gentle man he was. She said she loved him and then recounted his tragic death for me. He was on a plane that seated 4. He had begged to be allowed to go on the plane with the others, saying he was skinny enough to squeeze in. The plane ran out of fuel and crashed. Buddy was the only one who lost his life.

Several things happened for me in that same year. Adjusting to junior high school was a challenge but a lot of fun. Instead of one teacher all day long, we got to change classes 7 times a day and had 7 different teachers. That was cool in one way but hectic in another. It is hard to please seven masters.

English was always a breeze for me. I was never athletic and my skill in mathematics leaves a lot to be desired. (For the latter, I do have somewhat of an excuse. When I left Baltimore for my last year of elementary school in Allentown, the math teachers were just starting to teach fractions and long division. When I got to Allentown, they had just finished that. So I never really learned those skills, and they still haunt me sometime.) As for physical education, I just tried to hide in the woodwork most of the time. So, as can be easily predicted, my grades in English and Social Studies were good; math, science and physical education not great, but always passable. Art was never good for me; music was always good. Industrial Arts? That was like Art...so we can cross that one off, too. I could not hammer a nail straight to save my life, and I still can't. Guess what? Neither could my Dad. We were both glad that sister Sandy was around; she could! I am willing to bet that was no problem for Doris, but that mundane subject is something that we never discussed.

As Doris continued to put out more and more new records, my collection was growing in leaps and bounds. Before long, others were added to the collection.....Peggy Lee, Perry Como and Frank Sinatra, among them. Fortunately, two things helped in the spending money department. Besides going to school, I had two part-time jobs, both of which I kept throughout junior and senior high school. I worked at what was at that time called Riddell's. He was a jeweler and a candy maker. The store had three rooms. The front was divided into three parts; the jewelry counter on one side, the ice cream, milkshake and snowball counter across the back, and the candy counter was located on the opposite side.

Bernie (Mr. Riddell) was the original Jack of All Trades, Master of All! And me? Except for the jewelry counter, I helped with almost everything else. I sold candy, dipped ice cream, made snowballs and milkshakes. In the middle room was where we made the candy in large urns. I helped with that, too. The back was where we molded chocolate bunnies and Santas, where we dipped chocolate candies, and where we packed the candy into boxes for sale or storage. I did all that, too. We could eat as much candy and ice cream as our hearts desired; I got sick of both very quickly. Today, this candy maker is well known in the Baltimore County Area as *Log Cabin Candies*. I doubt that Mr. Riddell still runs it because he would be well into his 90's. I am sure the candy has not changed. It was the best in Baltimore back then.

The other part time job was my favorite. About five blocks from where I lived was where I purchased my records. It was a store called Monumental Appliance. The owner, Mr. Walter Wolosz, was a skilled technician in radio and TV. His base of operations was a back room and a cellar workshop. The main part of the store was devoted to the sale of records. I had been in and out of the store so often that when Mrs. Wolosz asked if I would like to work there, I literally jumped at the chance. Because I was not really old enough to work, we had to figure out the problem of how I would be basically compensated. We reached an amicable solution: she would pay me 10 single records and 2 albums a week. I was in 7th Heaven. Believe me, I never realized at the time that this would become such an expensive habit which I have had all my life. If you get that many free records every week, for all those years, you pretty much have all the music you want, and then some. But after working all those years in a record store, I got in the habit of having whatever music I wanted; it became way too costly after I no longer got them for free. My house has records everywhere.

There were some weeks that I didn't really want anything, and that is when my friends got little presents here and there. I had, at one time, so many records and albums that I literally did not have places to keep them. It was a sad day when I sold my entire 45-rpm collection (except anything by Doris which I still have.) I had about 5000 of them and no place to store them. I sold some of my albums, too, but not many. I still have too many of those and way too many CDs. I am proud to say that I own everything that was ever released by Doris on single records, albums or tapes. (And since the advent of computers and the internet, I also have anything that is available from there that was not in my personal collection, including some things never released as well.) I know it sounds insane, but if I had to skip lunch once in a while in order to purchase a prize by Doris, I never gave it a second thought. I still feel the same way. When the Baer Family Boxed sets of her music came out years later, I happily spent the dollars to get the golden treasures (each ran close to $200). They are under lock and key in my den closet. In that respect, Doris and I are similar. She keeps the recordings of her music hidden away, too, I am told…but in her case, I think she is not interested in hearing it. In my case, I want no one touching it.

At the times when I have had to move from place to place in my life, the only complaint I ever got from moving companies was about "those damn records!" (I let them move everything *except* the 78-rpms, which I still coddle. And of course I moved the Doris Day records myself, too.) With the exception of two bathrooms and a kitchen, every room of my current two-floor home houses some portions of my vast record collection. I would not part with it for anything, and if I could, I would take it with me when I go! Music has been the most consistent source of pleasure my entire life, and Doris Day is what has occupied the large majority of my listening time ever since I began collecting.

A Brief Diversion

I have to admit that I have had many favorite female singers over the years, even though none of them has come close to my affection for Doris. At times, this was a real conflict for me. A few good examples: "Confess" by Doris with Buddy Clark (the flip side of their #1 million-selling "Love Somebody") was also hitting the charts in 1948; it peaked at #16. Patti Page, however, gave them stiff competition on that song because her version peaked at #12. I have given that version many listens, and I have to admit, I can't stand it. That was not the only time that Patti gave Doris a jolt. In 1951, Doris paired with Harry James on a great version of a Top Ten Tune called "Would I Love You, Love You, Love You", complete with trumpet and Latin beat. It was the flip side of a gigantic jukebox hit, "Lullaby of Broadway". It, too, was a big jukebox hit and peaked on the charts at #10. But Patti's version of the same song reached #4. Again, I can't explain it because I think her interpretation of the song was weak in comparison. In those two instances, the competition made me want to break the Patti Page records. But giving Patti her due, no one can touch her versions of "Allegheny Moon", "Old Cape Cod", "The Tennessee Waltz", or "I Went To Your Wedding". A little irony here. Patti had a big hit with "How Much Is That Doggie in the Window". Those who seek it on the internet will find that, nine times out of ten, the artist which is erroneously listed is Doris Day. I doubt that Doris has ever sung the song at all, but knowing how well she always did with a novelty song (think "A Guy is A Guy" and "Purple Cow"), I have no doubt that a version by her would have given Patti a run for the money. In interviews in later years, Patti has said that Doris was always one of her personal favorites. And in Doris' most recent CD collection, *My Heart*, there is a song on the CD in which the vocal gives a nod to Patti Page and "Old Cape Cod".

Another thing that griped me was records that kept Doris from having the song spotlight as long as I thought she should (you know, like forever...). One of these was when "Que Sera, Sera" was in the Top Ten. It was a gigantic hit; it is still Doris' most remembered song (unfortunately). I say that only because there are so many better ones for which she should be

76

remembered. Anyway, when it was climbing the Top Ten on the charts (at least in *Billboard Magazine*), it never reached any higher than #2. Why is that? Because Elvis Presley's "Hound Dog" would not give it an inch. To this day, I cannot stand that record by Elvis (although I do like most of his work). It should not have mattered because in the end "Que Sera, Sera" ended up being a much bigger hit (both on the jukeboxes and for posterity). It also won the Academy Award for the Best Song of the Year. Another irony here. There was talk in the last few years before he died about a possible duet album for Doris and Elvis. What a treat that would have been. Just think of how well their voices would have blended. In two future albums, Doris sang tributes to Elvis by singing some of his most popular songs, including: "I Can't Help Falling in Love", "Are You Lonesome Tonight" and "A Fool Such As I".

On the other hand, I was always happy when her records beat out those who tried to cover her hits. Some come to my mind very quickly. One is 1954's "If I Give My Heart To You". Doris had the biggest version of that one, but some "one hit wonder" by the name of Denise Lor actually reached #8 with her version of the song. If you ever

77

hear that version, even you will wonder why. A few years later, Doris' friend, Kitty Kallen, did a revival of the song and brought it back to the Top 20. You can't keep a good song down.

Similarly, in 1949, Doris had a gigantic hit in "Again". Three other versions competed with hers: one by Gordon Jenkins, one by Mel Torme, and one by Vic Damone. I actually liked all of them, but no one can touch the majesty of the one by Doris and the Mellowmen. And although the other three versions may have hit the charts, the only one I ever saw on a jukebox was the one by Doris, deservedly so. This happened again with "When I Fall in Love". Doris' version was the first and most popular even though Nat King Cole tried to give her a run for the money. (I am glad it didn't work.)

And while I am very happy that research shows she is the biggest female seller of albums from the 1950's, including the #1 album of 1955 -- the soundtrack from the MGM film, *Love Me or Leave Me* -- Doris' #1 single records are few. Of course, this depends on your source. If one uses *Billboard Magazine*, they only give her that nod for two of them on her own, "Secret Love" and "A Guy is A Guy". (That does

not count her years with Les Brown or duets
with other artists.) Fortunately, there are
other sources who disagree. Using all of the
research sources combined, the list becomes
not two but eleven. The unfair thing here is
that when all-time records are tallied, #1
songs get the biggest nod, and the others
tend to be forgotten. Just one more example
of how Doris has often been slighted in her
career, and yes, it makes me angry.

The same thing is true about her movies.
Obviously, something has kept her in the
position of being the All-Time Female Box
Office Champion. No one has equaled that
record, and she comes in at #6 overall. No
female star in history has been #1 for four
years in a row, like Doris, nor maintained a
position in the Top Ten for as many years as
she. The records also show that she never
had a box office flop...all of the movies
made money, and some were the top money-
makers for their company in a given year.
And yet, too often, her body of work is
summarily dismissed, just as she was
slighted for what should have been two
Oscar nods and wins: her performances in
"*Love Me or Leave Me*" and "The Man
Who Knew Too Much". Some folks also
throw in that frenetic performance in
"Midnight Lace" as well. Tom Santopietro,

in his recent book, *Considering Doris Day*, tried to get the record straight. It makes me happy when some organizations take note. Here are just a few:

1962 - Golden Globe:
     World's Favorite Actress
1989 - Golden Globe: Cecil B. DeMille
     For Lifetime Acting Achievement
1991 - Lifetime Comedy Award
1998 - Grammy Hall of Fame for
     "Sentimental Journey"
1999 - Grammy Hall of Fame for
     "Secret Love"
2004 - Presidential Medal of Freedom
2008 - Grammy Lifetime Achievement
     Award for Excellence in Music
2010 - Legend Award from Society of
     Singers
2011 - Grammy Hall of Fame for
     "Que Sera, Sera"
2011 - Los Angeles Film Critics
     Lifetime Achievement Award

Check out the much longer list on her website, www.dorisday.com. All of these are well-deserved. My thought is that too many came too late, and some that should be there (Oscar, where are you?) are still among the missing. It took the Grammy Organization 30 years to catch up!

And now...off my soapbox, and back to the story. Thanks for your indulgence.

CHAPTER TEN:

END OF A DECADE

The forties ended on a top note for Doris and for me. In my case, it was the first of two years in junior high school. For Doris, it was two more top-rated films, *My Dream is Yours* (one of my very favorites) and *It's a Great Feeling* (with a star-studded cast of many Warner Brothers top stars in cameo bits including Joan Crawford and Errol Flynn). On records, Doris hit the Top Twenty often this year, and one of her biggest hits mid-year was called "Again". This one reached the top of the charts and was a consistent jukebox seller. Doris did many songs with a group called The Mellowmen as backup, and they blended well together. I loved the harmony. (Years later, I met one of the guys who used to sing with this group. He had nothing but praise for the singer he used to back. He said: "She was simply, the best." That was no surprise to me. No one who has ever worked with

Doris in the business has anything but praise.)

Two of Doris' other records from 1949 hold special memories for me. "Bluebird On Your Windowsill" was my baby sister Sandy's favorite, and we played it and played it and played it for her (always by request). It is one of those records on which Doris talks ("look at him out there, ain't he pretty"), and we all got a kick out of that. (note: even former English teacher me said nothing about the use of the word "ain't"…it wasn't important.) I also like the flip side which did not get as popular as "Bluebird", but it, too, was well represented on the air and on the jukeboxes. I always thought the French Nation should have taken a real interest in that one which was called "The River Seine". It was all about the river and its love for the City of Paris. If nothing else, it could have been a great advertisement for tourism.

The other song was a record I alluded to earlier on. It was a song from the Betty Hutton movie, *Red Hot and Blue*, and I know that Betty had a recording of it on the market, too. But it was Doris who made it a hit. The song was "(Where Are You) Now That I Need You". Between my mother, my sister Dolores and me, we wore out at least four copies of this one. We literally played it to death. Back then, records were all cardboard based and covered in shellac. The grooves were then cut into the shellac, and the needle played the grooves. If you played a record too much, you wore the shellac away. The records could still be played but needles could be destroyed, especially if there were gaping holes on the surface. Yes, I still have one of those original 78-rpm copies of this song complete with a gaping hole down to the cardboard. I could not bear to throw it away.

After her first movie, I didn't think I would ever see a Doris film I would like any better, but she has proved me wrong many times. I still love *Romance* because it was her first movie, and it was so good, but *My Dream is Yours* was pretty special, too. Like the first, it was another of the stories in which Doris played a young hopeful trying to become a star, as was movie #3. What made this one so different was the special relationship she had with the young star that played her son, sort of a reflection of her own life. So Art reflects life, they say. In the film, and in life, Doris had a young son to raise while she was building a career. And the truly special moment in the film, for me, came when Doris sang that wonderful song as a lullaby to her son, "I'll String Along With You". As my mother said when she saw it, "if that scene doesn't make you cry, you don't have a heart." I remember being a bit disappointed though when the record was released as a single. Instead of the beautiful lullaby that it was in the film, it became a love song duet for Doris with Buddy Clark. Of course, I realize that, at the time, there was no holding back on the dual hits for Doris and Buddy; it was just that this song really should have been a single just for Doris. Listen to the soundtrack sometime and you will see what I mean if you can compare the two versions. I hasten to add that even then commercialism played its card; the Clark/Day version could definitely have been the bigger hit, but true Doris fans would immediately know which one was the best version.

My Dream is Yours featured another big highlight for me. In the story, Doris' friends are looking out for her and trying to help her along. She works in a studio that plays songs for jukeboxes. I am not really sure, to this day, how that worked, unless it was really supposed to be some kind of live jukebox. At any rate, at one point Jack Carson (as the Hollywood agent) is looking for a new voice for a radio show. The bar patrons get him to listen to the jukebox as Doris sings along from a remote area. And the song was *"Canadian Capers (I Heard You Call For An All-Star Band)"*. This one was a gigantic jukebox favorite, and another favorite of mine as well. Everyone thought the title song from this film would be a big hit; it wasn't, but the title song of film #3, *It's A Great Feeling*, was nominated for an Academy Award. I wanted it to win (just like I did "It's Magic" in 1948). Its major contenders were: "Lavender Blue", "My Foolish Heart", "Through a Long and Sleepless Night", and the winner, "Baby, It's Cold Outside". "Great Feeling" as a song made you feel good, but as was almost always the case, Doris got slighted once again. It was a Top Hit, but no Oscar. That was yet to come a few years down the road. In fact, in 1956 Doris had two songs at the same time nominated for an Academy Award; one of them won.

I wrote to Doris quite a few times in 1949. She responded back with studio cards that contained her picture, which she always signed *"To Michael fondly Doris Day"*. I kept waiting for a letter, but I knew she was way too busy for that. And by then I was just one of many fans; Doris Day in the 50's and 60's got more fan mail than almost any other female star in Hollywood. And it may have taken a while, but Doris always responded in some way to every fan letter she ever got. As for letters, she did respond to one of my letters in which I asked her to record two of my favorite songs. Her letter read:

"Dear Michael

We will do our best and if it is at all possible I will be glad to record I'm in the Mood for Love and I Love All The Things You Are.

Thanks for your continued interest in my career and Keep listening and I will keep singing.

God bless you and all my fans.

Sincerely
Doris Day"

It was a bit on the formal side, but she responded, it was handwritten and it was definitely her handwriting. It went right into that scrapbook I started a few years earlier, and it was soon time for scrapbook #2. The first was getting jam-packed with cuttings from newspapers and magazines. It was hard to keep up with all of those because there were so many, but I tried. And the scrapbooks have some 8x10 glossy photos signed by Doris that I have never seen anywhere else (true collector's items). Funny...I never even gave a thought to joining or organizing a Doris Day Fan Club, but then, I wasn't the only one. She had fan clubs, but unbelievably, they were primarily in the United Kingdom, Australia and Germany, which is why, even today, Doris has a special affinity for her fans in the UK who have remained loyal throughout the years. It also explains why in 2011, a new CD (*My Heart*) featuring unreleased songs from the 80's was released in the UK. As I write these pages, it still has not been released in the US, but it is a top seller in the UK and reached #1 on the Amazon UK charts of top sellers.

As the 40's ended and a new decade began, Doris was undoubtedly one of the most popular female stars in the world...not just her movies but her records as well. And she was becoming one of the top performers in many venues: radio, records, movies, in person. From band singer and early dancing star, she had climbed to the top. And I smile as I write this, because I followed her most of the way. Every success made me very happy. It still does. Every disappointment made me sad. I say that because I doubt that it mattered to Doris. She has said she never kept track of which songs or movies were big hits or whatever; she enjoyed the process but was mostly uninterested in the results. She always tried to give the project one hundred percent, and that shows in all of her efforts. That may explain why she does not like to watch her movies or listen to her records today. She is afraid she will hear or see something that she would not like. Her fans never saw or heard anything they didn't like. And when so-called critics panned one of her efforts, we just wanted to kill them. When I mention her name, my friends tolerantly smile and silently think "not again"…they have heard me talk about Doris before.

CHAPTER ELEVEN:

THE FABULOUS FIFTIES BEGIN

Different people have some very different reactions to the two words "fabulous fifties". For some, it represents the advent of rock and roll and all things Elvis Presley, Bill Haley, Ricky Nelson, Fats Domino and the numerous other personalities that began the rock and roll era in the mid-fifties. For me, the Fabulous Fifties actually began in 1950 and were almost over by 1955 or so, when the rock generation sort of took over. It was the time when the big bands no longer dominated the world of music, but when male and female singers took over, and to some extent male and female groups (like the Four Aces) came to the fore. Most of the vocalists had been big band singers; now they were the primary focus, and the bands were used as background. It was the time of big names like Jo Stafford, Don Cornell, Frank Sinatra, Peggy Lee, Teresa Brewer,

Patti Page, Perry Como, Eddie Fisher and, of course, Doris Day, who ruled the airwaves.

I started 1950 with a "triple play"! Yes… unbelievably, I heard from Doris three times in a two week period. The first two times were 4x6 glossy signed pictures with a personal note. The third time was the charm. It was an 8x10 glossy signed on both back and front, one of my all-time favorite pictures of Doris. Evidently, I had written to Doris asking for some information on some of her older records. The back of the photo had this message:

"Michael dear

If you write to Columbia Records, Bridgeport Conn, they will be happy to give you all that information. Thanks for your sweet letter. Keep listening and I will keep singing.

God bless you.

Sincerely
Doris Day"

On the front was a typical pose of Doris from the 50's in which she is wearing three strands of pearls and a beautiful black dress.

It was signed *"To Michael fondly Doris Day."* Here is that picture:

Those three items began my second scrapbook which I titled "These Are The Things I Love". I heard from Doris at least eleven more times during the course of 1950 and early 1951, and I have the signed photographs to prove it. A funny thing, Doris never dated her photos or her letters. And I would never write on them; that would be like a sacrilege! But the photos are placed in the scrapbook and surrounded by ads and magazine articles all relating to things from 1950/1951. To this day, her correspondence to me is still mostly undated. Only the canceled stamp on the envelope has a mostly unreadable date. I guess that makes it more timeless, just like Doris.

Doris also released her first album collection in 1950; it was called *You're My Thrill*, and it contained seven classical ballad standards, and one song from the Broadway musical, *Pal Joey*. That one was released as a single and became one of her top hit parade songs of the year, "Bewitched". While I loved that, its flip side is one of the most beautiful recordings Doris ever made, and her voice on the song "Imagination" is truly the voice of an angel. I have that original set of 78-rpm records in a bound album containing the four single records in a kind of book. A few years later, it came out on 10" record and later with four songs added on a 12" album. I have all three. Like I have said before, I have far too many records.

I was definitely not a typical teenager of that time. I was not out playing various sports; in fact, I was hiding away from them. I never liked athletic anything and to this day I hate it when those kinds of events interfere with usual schedules (like TV shows or then radio shows). Personally, I think of many professional athletes as immature adults still playing kiddie games for which they receive far too much money. The only events of that nature I followed were the Olympic Events every four years. I also tended to like swimming events and ice skating (in their place -- not if they usurped other things in my preferred schedule). For some reason which I have never understood, physical education was a class required of all students every year including the first two years of college. If anything, it was a bother at whatever time of day it occurred. One had to change clothes into gym clothes, go to the gym or outside field, do a few startup exercises, play a 20-minute game of some sort or other, go back inside, shower, change back into school clothes and get on with the day, all in a period of 45 minutes. And during that time, those who were athletically inclined got to show off, while those of us who were less skilled got to be ridiculed for said lack of skills. In high school, for two years, I had a different kind of teacher for this course, and I was forever grateful. On the first day, he divided the class into those who enjoyed sports and those who didn't. For us non-enthusiasts, he provided an opportunity to play volleyball, tennis, badminton or Dodge Ball...none of which required exceptional athleticism. And we never had to be ridiculed by the show offs.

There needed to be a lot more coaches like him. In Doris' world, it would not have mattered because from all I have seen, she is certainly one of those who is athletically inclined.

At home in the evenings after work, I did a lot of radio listening. I don't want to give the impression that there was really a lot to watch; television was just getting started. And there were not many channels once it did: it was cowboys, Uncle Miltie and Arthur Godfrey or nothing, for the most part, and Howdy Doody for my sister. I recall lots of radio listening but not a lot of TV watching. It was great fun to be scared by the *Molle Mystery Theater* and *The Shadow Knows* and on Saturday Mornings, we never seemed to be too old to "*Let's Pretend*".

The first time I ever heard one of my all-time favorite Doris songs, "If I Give My Heart To You", was on *Peter Potter's Jukebox Jury.* They would play new records and vote them a hit or a miss. A panel of five made the decision. This one they called a unanimous hit, and they were right. They also pronounced the flip side, "Anyone Can Fall in Love", a hit as well. It was a hit but not as big a hit as the A side. I could not wait to get it, and when it came out, I bought three copies…this is one I knew I would wear out.

I remember being busy in this first year as a teenager, but mostly being busy working at the candy or record stores. I was not out playing like everyone else. I spent an inordinate amount of time in my room playing Doris records because my folks always kept asking me to turn it down. I had a couple of friends but none close enough that we spent any great amount of time together. And that goes all the way back to my earliest childhood. I do not recall any truly close friends, male or female. My closest friends were family members... not a bad thing. Unlike other teenagers of the time, I did not have a close bosom buddy; I wish I had but that was not the case. That did not happen until later in high school and college. I also have to admit I do not recall doing much homework (that came when I got to college). I do recall one time when my mother got a call from one of my teachers who was worried that I was working too hard. She seemed to think that my IQ did not correlate to the kinds of grades I was getting and was worried that I was working my tail off for countless hours in order to do so. My mother was shocked and told the teacher, "I never ever see him doing any homework of any kind." Funny, I don't remember spending much time on homework, but it did get done, and I managed to get acceptable grades (mostly *C's* and *B's*, with an occasional *A*). So much for IQ! And also for meddlesome teachers (something I never became.)

I never got tired of my job at the music store, and by this time, Mr. Wolosz had rigged up a speaker to one of the turntables in house, so I could serenade the entire neighborhood. Naturally, they heard a lot of Doris records! Our store was one of the biggest sellers in the area of Doris Day records. I wonder why? Back in those days, when people came in to buy a new single, it was our policy to play it for them first unless they asked us not to do so. If they asked for recommendations, you know who I always suggested first, every time. I especially remember pushing many, many copies of "Mr. Tap Toe". I was happy that I had the job in the store when I did…a few years earlier, it would have been the big band sound, and that was not my favorite. I got there when the Fabulous Fifties vocalists were in vogue, and I loved most of them from Doris to Perry Como and Eddie Fisher to Peggy Lee and all in between. Today, my tastes in music remain the same: I prefer the vocalists to the instrumentalists, but I throw in the great groups as well (Four Aces/Four Lads) and hundreds of others, as well as the period of the great American folk singers, like The Kingston Trio and The Brothers Four.) And I don't rule out little known groups today that were big then like The Four Preps, The Hilltoppers, and The Gaylords.

Doris had three hit movies in 1950. In the first, she played a band singer who became a famous vocalist in *Young Man With A Horn,* certainly a reflection of her own career. It was her first movie filmed in black and white; I have no idea why. I would have preferred color. But that did not stop me from loving the movie, although I could not fathom one of its co-stars, Lauren Bacall, someone I still consider highly over-rated. Besides, Lauren got the man (Kirk Douglas) when he tossed Doris aside. ABSURD! This movie did give Doris her first chance to record with Harry James, his trumpet, and his orchestra, and what a great pairing it was. First off, it generated a Top Ten hit single of "Would I Love you, Love You, Love You" and the flip side which is unquestionably one of Doris' best single records, a brilliant interpretation of "The

Lullaby of Broadway", which also just happened to be the title of one of her biggest movies of 1951. *Horn* gave her the chance to vocalize on four songs from the film: "The Very Thought of You", "With A Song in My Heart", "Too Marvelous For Words" and an up-tempo version of "I May Be Wrong (But I Think You're Wonderful)". These songs were paired with four instrumental sides by the Harry James Orchestra and became a #1 best-selling album in 1950.

The other two movies in 1950 co-starred her most consistent fellow trooper, Gordon MacRae. They made a great pairing and appeared in 5 films as co-stars. *Tea For Two* was a take-off on a Broadway show called *No, No, Nanette*. It was a nostalgic musical set in the 1920's with some great old-time tunes. I was very excited for Doris in this film. One of her co-stars was dancer Gene Nelson, and she got to finally dance once again. This was her original intended career; she thought she would never dance again. But dance she does, and as well as any other female dancer that I have ever seen on the big screen. This only added to her musical talents and what she could accomplish in future films. This movie also afforded Doris another top selling album that year.

The West Point Story was exactly as its title implied. Doris played a Hollywood star that was coerced into appearing in a West Point musical by a former show business friend, played by James Cagney (who would be her costar a few years later in one of Dodo's career highlights). Her other co-stars were Gordon MacRae, Virginia Mayo and Gene Nelson. This was another of her movies filmed in black and white. I really do not understand the reason for this one either. If Warner's was trying to compete with MGM in the big movie musical department, black and white was not the way to go.

The big song from this musical was called "You Love Me" and it was a duet for its two stars. It did not have a chance to become a big hit on the charts because it was never released as a duet; Doris and Gordon were on different record labels. It could have been a hit for Doris and Buddy Clark, but he was no longer with us. C'est La Vie.

This year was important to me for another reason. As a 13-year old, I was now a teenager and could go to the weekend teen centers. We met every Friday or Saturday night at a local elementary school, in the gym or activities room. There, we socialized with others of our age, and the teen center leaders were usually two adults unrelated to any of the teenagers present. We played games (not sports), learned how to dance, and danced. I met many fast friends at these dances, friends who are still part of my circle today. They all knew that I worked in a record store, so I was officially elected as "Guardian of the Music". I had a gigantic metal box with a handle that held forty 78-rpm records, which I would carry back and forth each week. I still have it; it is big and Hunter Green in color. (When records started to be produced on the 45-rpm with the big hole in the middle, I had boxes that would hold 100 records.) At the teen center, I got to spin the records, announce the songs, play lots of Doris Day, and even had a Top Twenty countdown every week. Doris always had one or two or more songs in the Top 20 because the guys at the teen center got to vote, and I tended to help influence the voting. Not cheating, you see, just a little strong persuasion. One of Doris' biggest teen center songs was one that most people have never heard. It was called "You Have My Sympathy", and it was #1 for seven weeks at the teen center. I don't recall ever hearing it on the radio. I am sure that those who attended the teen center will remember it still. It was a great ballad and a good song with which to do a slow dance. Once the movie came out in 1951, *I'll See You in My Dreams* was our weekly close-out song and the last dance of the evening until we graduated from high school and stopped attending. Funny how we stuck to the norms. You were a teenager when you turned 13, but suddenly that stopped as soon as you graduated from high school and became a young adult…we wouldn't be caught dead at a teen center then.

This is the time when I started gathering close friends. It had everything to do with two things: my records and the fact that I was considered to be a good dancer. The fact that we rode the same school bus to and from school each day had nothing to do with it because the bus was so packed from front to back that we rarely ever had a chance to talk. In high school, once I got my own car that changed as I carried from 5 to 6 people to and from school those years. I meet almost every year with some of these folks in an annual fall excursion to Ocean City, Maryland, where we just enjoy each other's company. Some still live close by but others are as far away as California and Florida.

It's great to get together. And all my friends knew I was a Doris Day junkie…so it was kind of like: Love Me/Love Doris. They complied. Today, some of them love Doris almost as much as I do. I said some. The others have learned how to tolerate my fanaticism.

One of these forever friends is a bulwark with the Republican Party in Maryland. She lost her bid for Governor in a close race several years ago. I bring her up because we were both attuned to dancing in high school and we both liked Doris. We even learned how to do some outrageous dances like the tango and the rhumba. But mostly we jitterbugged. We had other school mates who always joined us at the school dances, especially when the people in charge announced a dance contest. It was usually a jitterbug, and most of the time, it ended with the same two couples up for the finish, one couple or the other winning at different times. There was Joe and Arlene, Ellen and me. (We called her "Winkie", but we won't get into that except to say that she had gorgeous eyes.)

CHAPTER TWELVE:

1951 - FIVE HITS FOR DORIS;
HIGH SCHOOL FOR MIKE

Entering high school in 1951 was not a
traumatic experience. We went from a
dilapidated old brick building into a modern,
fashionable and fairly new one perched on a
hill. We went from traversing two floors
with lunch in an old classroom, to a school
with three floors and a real cafeteria. It may
have only been ninth grade, but back then, it
was the first year of high school, even
though we were lowly freshmen (that's only
the first time…we were to be that again once
we got to college).

I liked high school because I really got
involved with all kinds of activities.
There were several special teachers for me
there, too. Miss Shores was really tough;
getting a "C" from her was like getting an
"A+" from anyone else. She was a stickler

for grammar and punctuation and spelling, and they became favorites of mine, too. She made me work my tail off, and I loved it. It paid off because I got an "A" in English that year. Later, in my junior year, when it was time to select colleges and careers, my plan was to go into business for myself (Dad thought that I should try to manage a record shop. He and Mom could definitely not afford to send me to college). Miss Shores would not hear of it. She insisted that I go to college, took me herself to the guidance counselor where they had me fill out all kinds of forms so that I could apply for a college scholarship. In my senior year, I was offered a full scholarship to Towson State Teachers College, and because of Miss Shores, I majored in English and graduated from college with an A average, four years later. But I am moving too far down the road at this juncture.

Another special high school teacher for me was Mrs. Reimensnyder. Another English teacher, she also taught Journalism. I took Journalism as an elective, and liked it so much that I took it throughout high school, eventually becoming Business Manager and Features Editor for the school newspaper, sponsored by Mrs. R. She was a fun lady and everyone enjoyed being around her. A perusal of the school papers for the three years on which I served show many mentions of Doris Day, her movies and her music. As many of you probably know, high school schedules often included a study hall one or two periods a week (often to fill in the periods when a student has a subject like art or music or other minor subjects that only meet three days a week.) Since it was always a five-day week, the schedule had to be filled in for those two periods. I got bored easily in study halls; I, fortunately, did not really need them. So, I talked Mrs. R. into letting me spend those periods with her working on the school paper. It happened to coincide with her free period. Because of that, we became truly good friends. We talked about everything under the sun… Doris Day included. Yes, Mrs. R. was a fan, too. She also insisted on my going to college. She wanted me to major in Journalism. I didn't, but I served on the college newspaper all four years and ended up being Assistant Editor-in-Chief. As a matter of fact, when I was ready to graduate from college and was assigned a teaching position in Baltimore County, I got my first choice of schools because I agreed to sponsor the school newspaper in a junior high school.

Another high school teacher had a significant effect on me. Her name was Mrs. Beck, whom I had for eleventh grade English. It was she who gave me my love for literature and composition. She encouraged us to write about many things, especially things that we knew and things that were important to us. On my first composition, I wrote about Doris. It was the first time I ever received an A+ on an English composition, but it was not the last. She told me that I had a good style of writing and that what I wrote was always correct in grammar, punctuation and spelling. She said that she also enjoyed reading about her favorite movie star. I was happy she liked my writing because I got straight A's in English that year, and on the report card for the end of the year, she actually filled in a plus after the A. To my knowledge, that was not a regular feature. I was told she actually had to go to my homeroom teacher's room the day report cards were distributed and fill it in by hand to make sure that it got there. What a surprise! She, too, was insistent that I go to college and become a teacher. I think the three English teachers were in cahoots; they got the job done! And I never regretted either decision: going to college or even becoming a teacher.

Then there was Miss Ainsley. She taught Music. She encouraged me to sing and by senior year, I was a member of the All School Chorus. We sang the songs at the graduation ceremonies. Miss Ainsley was primarily interested in classical music and older standards. She was unfamiliar with Doris Day. In her case, I made her a convert, but I started her off with "Till My Love Comes To Me" (from *Young at Heart*) because it had a classical theme. Then I brought in other music by Doris, and she loved it! She was tickled the day I brought her a Doris album as a present. Her influence led me to become a member of the College Glee Club when I got to Towson State Teacher's College (now Towson University). I also ended up singing around campus with two other guys when we formed a three tenor trio. We called ourselves "The Three D's" (Don, Digger and DeVita, the D's in our respective names.) To this day, when it is not Doris singing, I love listening to a choir or group with full harmony. The Chordettes and The Four Aces are special favorites from the 50's. I am also fond of The Ten Tenors and Il Divo. And I still like to sing and harmonize with others. Some of my favorite Doris records are ones in which sings with herself in harmony ("Kiss Me Goodbye, Love", "Jimmy Unknown", and others.)

For Doris, 1951 was a banner year...She appeared in five, count 'em, five films. What other star can we mention who has ever done so many films in one year? I can't think of any. And today, I doubt that any star would do that many films in one year. It is rare if they do two. Sadly, times have changed.

The first of these movies was another black and white film, but this time for a good reason. It was called *Storm Warning*, and Doris co-starred with her childhood idol, Ginger Rogers. The movie is a story about the Klu Klux Klan, a very dark movie considering the subject. It is the only movie in which Doris dies at the end. There was also no singing. For me, that accounted for two disappointments. My heart skipped a beat when the movie ended; I could not believe they would kill off Doris. HOW HORRIBLE. I guess the movie served two good purposes. It exposed the KKK as an organization that needed to be controlled, and it was the first time that Hollywood directors got a chance to see that Doris could do a dramatic role if the occasion called for it (and probably influenced Director Alfred

Hitchcock to star her in *The Man Who Knew Too Much* a few years later.) My family and friends liked the movie but not nearly as much as we did the next one. Let me take that back, Mom loved it, but she was the only one who did.

The next one that we all loved was *Lullaby of Broadway,* one of my all-time Doris favorites. This time she co-starred with Gene Nelson. This is the film for which she did some highly acclaimed dancing. Other dancers still talk about her dancing up and down a high set of stairs in a long gold dress in high heels. Gene Nelson's wife, a dancer herself, said it is something she would never have done…much too dangerous. Doris didn't give it a second thought; she was dancing again and with a really well accomplished partner. Nelson never got the credit he deserved, but he was every bit as good as Astaire, Kelly and O'Connor. This movie holds one of several records for me. I saw it with everyone! My sister and I saw it, my mother and I saw it, I went with my neighborhood friends to see it. I think the total was eight times. No, I didn't see it 40 or 50 times like some fans; eight was a record for me. The music was truly wonderful and produced another #1 hit album for Doris, one of two that year. There were lots of great songs. The one touted to be a big hit, "I Love The Way You Say Good Night", was not. The big hit was the title song (not the version from the film with the Norman Luboff Choir, but the one she recorded in the studio with Harry James). It was not Top Ten on the *Hit Parade*, but it cleaned up on the jukeboxes, and fans and critics alike say it is one of Doris' best efforts. There were some great nostalgic songs (like "Shanty in Old Shanty Town" and "Somebody Loves Me"). Doris does a terrific song and tap dance routine to "Just One of Those Things", and sings one of my favorites in a song and dance with Nelson, "You're Getting To Be A Habit With Me". On the album, the last cut is called **"Please Don't Talk About Me When I'm Gone"**, and as she approaches the end of the song, she makes it sound like she is actually drifting off into the distance. Pretty cool!

During this time, Doris had two top ten singles. The first was the flip side of *Lullaby*, "Would I Love You", discussed earlier. That peaked at #10 and charted for ten weeks. On its heels was one that reached #7 on the charts and #1 on the jukeboxes, charting for 20 weeks. It was called "Shanghai". I loved it! And played it to death. (The flip side was a beautiful ballad that was a minor hit called "My Life's Desire", a perfect wedding song. You wedding planners should check it out sometime.) One of the signed picture cards I got from Doris that year had on the back an ad for many of her Columbia recordings. Doris herself penned in the title of the song "Shanghai"...she knew which was going to be the biggest hit! But one of her biggest hits of all time was coming...a year later.

Then it was time for Doris to star once again with Gordon MacRae in a wonderfully nostalgic turn of the century musical called *On Moonlight Bay*. This, too, was a box office hit, as were most of Doris' films. It came out in July, a good time for me, because I was visiting my aunts and uncles in Allentown, and three guesses where we were when we saw the movie. Yep, we were on an annual vacation excursion from Allentown to Atlantic City, and it was playing in one of the Boardwalk cinemas. We were all excited about seeing another great musical starring Doris. I was happy to share the viewing experience with Pippy and Anna Marie. In preparation for that big night, Anna Marie and Buddy had found this store that printed "select your own banner headlines" and presented me with a large newspaper that had as its title: *MIKE*

DEVITA DATES DORIS DAY. What a trip! It holds a place of honor in scrapbook #2 next to all the ads for the movie, which I loved. Everyone knows that Doris has a fabulous face when it comes to making gestures that can tell a whole story. This is especially true in one scene of the movie on a duet with Jack Smith, The song is called *"Love Ya, Honey"*. Her expressions had us in stitches, and the song became one of my favorites. It actually combines a ukulele with a jazz/ Dixieland beat. If you haven't heard it, you should find it and give it a listen. The album was another big seller for Doris Day. And the movie? It was a big box office hit. Critics have said the movie holds up well. It was Warner Brothers' answer to MGM's big movie musical, *Meet Me in St. Louis*. Personally, I like it better. Both make good family movies, both have a special Christmas time flavor, and both feature kids doing what kids do. I do like Judy Garland, and she has a good voice, and the songs in *St. Louis* were good ("Have Yourself A Merry Little Christmas", "The Boy Next Door", the Title Song, and "The Trolley Song"), but for me no one can compete with Doris. And *Bay* had some terrific old songs, too. I still have my bound 78-rpm album of the movie songs, including: "Till We Meet Again", "Cuddle

Up A Little Closer", "Every Little Movement" and the title song. *Bay* also had a special Christmas moment with the song called "The Christmas Story", complete with snow, trimmed tree, and carolers singing along. In addition, it had two new songs, a treat for Doris fans. "Tell Me" (a sad one) and "Love Ya, Honey", a great one. We liked the movie so much, we went to see it several more times when we got back home. I could never make a list of my favorite Doris movies because I like them all for different reasons, but if I was forced, this would have to be in my Top 20.

Doris' next two films in 1951 were both in black and white. I guess Warner Brothers had its reasons, but once again, to compete with MGM Musicals, color should have been the route. The first of these co-starred Danny Thomas. He was not my favorite co-star for Doris, but that did not matter. The black and white did not matter. Both seemed to work. The film set all kinds of box office records, especially at Radio City Music Hall in New York City. It was the biography of songwriter, Gus Kahn. Doris played his wife and biggest supporter. The songs were absolutely delightful, as was her second #1 top selling album for the year. Among others, it featured a song which

Doris has since dedicated twice, "My Buddy". The first time, she dedicated it to Rock Hudson after his death from AIDS on her cable television show, *Best Friends*. On her *My Heart* CD, she included this song dedicated to her son Terry, who died from Melanoma in 2004. Other great songs from the movie included: "Ain't We Got Fun", "It Had To Be You", "Nobody's Sweetheart", "Makin' Whoopee", "The One I Love", the title song, and a truly beautiful rendition of the song, "I Wish I Had A Girl". Certainly, it is an album worth owning, and one that I have worn out; that is especially true for the track "Wish I Had A Girl". I have the original 10" album release. Today, it is available on cd with the soundtrack from *Calamity Jane*, one heck of a good buy. I am one of those purists who think that the sound is still better on the vinyl recordings than it is on CDs available today, but that is strictly a matter of choice.

The fifth film for Doris in what had to be an exhausting year for her was called *Starlift*. It is only a Doris Day film because she is in it. And because she was in it is what gave it any success that it had at the box office. It grossed almost four million dollars on its initial release; that certainly is a nice chunk of change considering it was only 1951.

Doris plays herself in this movie, as do the other stars who appear in the film, including James Cagney, Gordon MacRae, Gene Nelson, Jane Wyman, Virginia Mayo, Ruth Roman and others. The movie was based on a Hollywood program called "Operation Starlift" created by the Special Service Officers and Hollywood Coordinating Committee to bring movie stars of the time to Travis Air Force Base in order to entertain the wounded coming in from the Korean War. Once Doris is no longer part of the film, after about 45 minutes, it lost all interest for me. However, it did produce a few gems. She duets with MacRae on "You're Gonna Lose Your Gal", a great pairing. And she sings three other songs: "S'Wonderful" (with a jukebox), "You Oughta Be in Pictures" and "You Do Something To Me". None of these performances were ever released on single records, and the movie was not even released until just recently for those who wanted to purchase it. While Doris is in the film, she lights up the screen. Once she is gone...goodbye movie. Doris fan or not, I am sure the viewer would agree. As a film, it was certainly not a great way to end the year for Doris, but as you will see, from a film point of view, her greatest successes were definitely not in 1951 and not in musical films.

Off the Record...

Scrapbook #3 has two 8X10 glossy photos that Doris sent me in 1951. The first is one of her on the floor of what looks like a living room. She is in front of a fireplace with a pile of papers in front of her and it looks like she is singing. The second is from the set of *Moonlight Bay*, where she is dressed in a baseball uniform and someone on the set is dusting her off with a broom. She autographed both of these pictures.

The first three scrapbooks which I have alluded to effectively take my "affair" with Doris from 1948 through 1951. All the pictures, letters and cards from Doris, magazine cutouts and other items relate specifically to those years, including one of her rare endorsement ads, this time for Royal Crown Cola. As I write this section, I am boxing these three scrapbooks with fear and trepidation in order to send them to my friend and fellow Doris Day FANatic, Carol in Georgia, so that she can do her work of restoration and preservation. Cross your fingers for me that they do not get lost in the mail!!! I trust her implicitly. I cannot say the same about the U.S. Postal Service. If I am still in the process of writing when these are returned, I will let you know, as I now move to 1952 and scrapbook #4.

Somewhere along the way, I began to get disassembled in my scrapbook collection because things in book #4 are definitely not in any kind of chronological order. I hope that was not a reflection of my life at the time.

The first item in it goes directly to 1959 (my last year in college and first year of teaching) and the second picks up in 1954…that is what I mean by lack of order. That is definitely not my usual style, as I have often been accused of being too orderly, to the point of anality, if you know what I mean. My motto has always been "a place for everything, and everything in its place, if you please". So, whatever happened to my sense of organization and decorum with the beginning of scrapbook #4 eludes me completely. I must have been totally oblivious at the time. I have no reasonable explanation..not even one that is insanely unreasonable. Nevertheless…onward we go.

As of October 28, 2011, Carol is now working on the DeVita/Doris Day Project

Scrapbook Restoration Process, you will be happy to hear. I will let you know how it turns out when I see it.

CHAPTER THIRTEEN:

"SHE WALKED DOWN THE STREET LIKE A GOOD GIRL SHOULD..."

In 1952, it was time for Doris to have her next #1 hit record, and believe me it was a monster hit. It charted for over five months, and along with another of her big records for that year, it was on jukeboxes for over a year. I refer to another of her million selling gold records, "A Guy is a Guy". I have said many times, and I will say it again. Doris Day can sing anything and make it sound good. From ballads and love songs, to up-tempo tunes, to songs that reflect a classical air, to actual jazz, to novelty songs. And everyone loved this one. Even today, when I play it if people are around, they sing along. It certainly was infectious and hugely popular.

This year, as in no other, is paramount in proving my point about the Day versatility. The big ballad of the year was called "When I Fall in Love". It has been recorded by every major star imaginable, but Doris had the first Top 20 version of that one, and it is her version that its composers prefer.

She had duets with almost every major Columbia star in the label stable. And all of them hit the charts, the biggest being her duet with Frankie Laine on "Sugarbush". That one was a scary experience for me. Pippy told me not to buy it because she was sending it in the mail. Send it she did. When I opened the package, I wanted to cry. It was all in little pieces. Who says a 10th grade boy does not cry. I was beside myself. The result was: various people tried to make me feel better by presenting me with a copy of the record. I ended up with 10 copies, including two more in the mail from Pippy.

Billboard charts say it reached #7 and charted for 14 weeks. It was in the Top Ten on the very first charted hit listing in the United Kingdom in 1952. On the jukeboxes…hmm…another story. I made sure it was on My Uncle Harry's jukebox in the bar in Allentown. He told me that every time he tried to replace it, customers complained. It was still there when he closed the bar in the 70's. At the time, I don't recall passing any jukebox where it was not the song being played. (very big smile)

Other popular recording duet partners for

Doris that year included: Guy Mitchell ("A Little Kiss Goodnight" and "Gently Johnny"), Donald O'Connor ("No Two People" and "You Can't Lose Me") and Johnny Ray ("A Full Time Job" and "Ma Says, Pa Says", a two-sided hit). Doris liked the last one so much that she sang it with all kinds of people all over the radio that year. The combination of Doris and Johnny Ray was so popular that they came back in 1953 with another chart topper in "Candy Lips" (the flip side was "Let's Walk Thataway").

This was the year that Doris starred in her own radio show. Remember, she had been on various other radio shows before this year, from Bob Hope to Al Jolson, etc. This time it was her own thing. That caused a bit of a problem for me. As an avid collector, I just knew she would sing songs that were not available to buy. And that put me in a quandary. I went to one of the stores near my home that sold reel-to-reel tape recorders. I begged and pleaded with the owner to let me purchase one, and I promised to pay it off weekly.

At first, it was on layaway. I think I promised to pay $5 a week. I don't recall how much it cost, but I am guessing at the time that it was probably close to one hundred dollars, quite a bit in 1952 dollars. I made enough at the candy store to be able to swing it. After four weeks of trudging there with my $5 in hand, the owner let me take it home in advance of payment. In the end, he knocked off the last $30 for my faithfulness. At the time, I could not have been happier. I was able to record the shows each week (or most of them) and had them on tape storage. I had no idea that tapes shrunk and got distorted with time. Today, I can't even play them. What a sad state of affairs that is. I know the powers to be have released two of the series on CD so far (roughly about eight shows), but that is as far as they have gone. They need to do more. They need to release it all. I have no idea why people hoard things. Things like this should be available to the public.

This show and the tape recorder caused a big argument one night with my father. I believe the show was broadcast initially on Friday evenings. In Baltimore, for some weird reason, it was broadcast around supper time on a Sunday evening. And of course, we were supposed to be eating at supper time. For me, that was a conflict. The first time I was set to record a show, my father yelled upstairs: "Time for dinner". I said, "I am recording the Doris Show". He won that argument. I missed the show. I did not speak to him for six days. And then, Mom solved the problem. Dinner on Sundays from then on came earlier or later…but I never missed the show again. Remember, Mom was a Doris fan too…and she wanted to hear the shows as well.

On the film front, Doris went from five films in 1951 down to two movies in 1952. Neither of these was one of her best films, but both did surprisingly well at the box office….after all, by now, Doris was a Top Ten box office star and a worldwide favorite. Everything she did at the time would do well. Her home studio, Warners, knew that well. They abused her talents all too often. But she brought in more fan mail at the studio than any other female star.

The first film in 1952 was with Ronald Reagan (yes, Mr. President) and Frank Lovejoy, *The Winning Team*. Doris played the wife of baseball great, Grover Cleveland Alexander, played by Reagan. It was another black and white movie for Doris at the height of her popularity. Any other studio would have capitalized on her talents; Warners took her for granted. She sang one song in the movie, "Ol' St. Nicholas", while decorating a Christmas tree. This movie grossed over 3.4 million in 1952 dollars so it was an official box office hit. It was another time that I personally was not thrilled with a Day co-star, but it would get worse before it got better. Reagan was never more than a "B" actor; Doris was better and deserved better especially at this point in her career.

A brief side note

Let's talk about Doris' co-stars. She began her career starring opposite Jack Carson who was never an A listed actor, and he wasn't the handsomest man in Hollywood. But the pairing worked for three films. Then came Kirk Douglas who was a good actor but for Doris the movie was truly only a supporting role after three in which she was top billed. Then it was time for Gordon MacRae. A winning combination. Ditto Gene Nelson. And then we have Danny Thomas. Next was Ronald Reagan, followed by Ray Bolger. By 1953, Warners wised up. Howard Keel to Rock Hudson and James Garner were definite improvements in the co-star department.

The other 1952 film for Doris grossed over 5.5 million dollars. It was called *April in Paris*. It was well publicized. But Doris fans (me included) just could not get it. RAY

BOLGER? Come on…after all, he was a scarecrow. The movie was disappointing. By this time, Doris was ready to show off both her dancing and singing. Ray was definitely a dancer but the film did not capitalize on those talents except in a brief scene with the song "I'm Gonna Ring The Bell Tonight" that takes place in a shipboard kitchen. The scene belonged to Doris, and I loved it. To this day, I cannot believe the scene in which Doris appears with four or five dogs all dyed in different colors of the rainbow. I can't believe she allowed that to happen. (Four years later, she was pulling rank on how animals were treated and got her way for *The Man Who Knew Too Much*). At any rate, *Paris* had some good moments, some fair songs, and one great one, of course, the title song. And no one sings it better than Doris. She makes you feel like you are experiencing Paris in springtime.

Correspondence with Doris from 1952 through 1955 was spotty at best. I can't say for sure, but I feel certain that because of her immense popularity, I am sure she had several people helping with fan mail. That would explain why so many responses from her, at the time, were pre-signed studio cards. I got many of those, but only one actually signed picture in that time span. On the other hand, that was a busy time for me as well. I was doing the high school thing, and that is always a busy time for a teenager who is also working. I never missed a new record. I never missed seeing a film, but there was not a lot of time to write back and forth for either of us. Doris continued, however, to dominate my bedroom where I listened to her records on a daily basis and had magazine pictures not pasted in scrapbooks all over the walls of my room.

CHAPTER FOURTEEN:

FROM SILVERY MOON AND CALAMITY JANE TO YOUNG AT HEART

Of course, 1953 was a great year for Doris fans. When *Moonlight Bay* ended a few years earlier, the co-stars as characters in the film were separated and intended to get married when he returned from war. So…the sequel was a long-time coming. It was great to see Doris and Gordon MacRae back together again (albeit for the last time). In fact, everyone from the first film returned except Jack Smith. So, the Winfield family was reunited in *By The Light of the Silvery Moon* and a great reunion it was. It was a fun movie with a fun, convoluted story. The songs were definite highlights, especially one called "Be My Little Baby Bumble Bee", and this was the second time in a movie that Doris sang "Ain't We Got Fun". (The first time was with Danny Thomas in

I'll See You In My Dreams; this time with Gordon MacRae.) The big production number was called "King Chanticleer" which has Doris cavorting with all kinds of barnyard characters. The great ballads from the film were "Your Eyes Have Told Me So" and "I'll Forget You". And Merv Griffin made his screen debut at the end of the movie in a bit part as a band leader while everyone ice skates off to the title tune. Truly a family film, and we all loved it. The album soundtrack reached #3 on the best-selling charts. We didn't know at the time, but the best was yet to come!

I have never been a fan of westerns or cowboy films. That said, *Calamity Jane* was an enjoyable film in every way possible, and Doris was undoubtedly the star of all stars. We thought she would be teamed with Gordon MacRae again, but that was not the case. We did not know at the time, but I have learned recently that he had a problem with alcohol and could not be relied on. Other stories say he was asking too much money. Who knows? It didn't matter; Howard Keel (a constant favorite on Broadway) was just perfect as Wild Bill Hickok. Doris had a cute, funny accent in the movie; the teaming was good. No one knows why they never appeared together again. (It was rumored that they were supposed to be the co-stars of "Unsinkable Molly Brown", but that never happened.) And although the script tried to make Doris look and sound unappealing, it didn't work in that way. We liked her even with a muddy face. And the songs....what truly wonderful songs. From the opening rouser "Deadwood Stage" to the song and dance routine in a barroom, "Just Blew in From the Windy City", all of them were fun to listen to and to sing along with. There was special magic in "A Woman's Touch". But the climax, of course, was the song for which Doris eventually won a Grammy Award, the very beautiful "Secret Love". The soundtrack album peaked at #2 but it was popular throughout 1953 and 1954. "Secret Love" was so popular that year. At the teen center, we played it two or three times an hour, by request…it was that popular. The same was true on area jukeboxes. It was on the radio every time I turned it on, and I loved it. As did everyone except one notorious Baltimore disc jockey/radio and TV show host by the name of Buddy Deane. He was more impressed with himself than anyone else was impressed by him. Those who lived in Baltimore in the 1950's who have seen the Broadway show or the movie version of *Hairspray* know that the plot loosely resembles the scene in Baltimore involving this horrid little man and his weekly television show.

I am not going to get into that except to say two things. When "Secret Love" was immensely popular all over the nation, Buddy Deane did not play it. (He NEVER played songs by Doris because he did not like her. What a jerk!) Anyway, I remember very clearly the day he did play this record. He said, over the air, and I quote: "Now that this record has become #1 nationally, I have to play it, so here is 'Secret Love' by Doris Day." Can you believe the gall?

One more little anecdote about Buddy Deane, and I will drop his name from memory forever. On the occasion of our 25th high school reunion, I had the job of inviting "people who were well known during our high school years" to our reunion. I invited everyone from Doris to Pat Boone and Rosemary Clooney to Buddy Deane. We got very nice "Thanks but we can't make it" notes from most of them, including Doris. From Pat Boone, we got a great poster, several pictures and a signed pair of white buck shoes (all door prizes that evening). Pat was always one of our favorites, and that made him just more so.

Clooney, to our surprise, never even acknowledged the letter (and she was appearing in a club locally at the time). The Four Lads sent us an autographed record to give away. We did hear from Buddy Deane, currently living in Virginia. He told us he would be happy to put in an appearance. Our cost would be $2,500 plus his airfare, hotel bill and car rental fees. We laughed a lot about that. What an arrogant individual. We were willing to give him his supper but no more. Today, *"Secret Love"* has become a real classic. It won both an Academy Award and a Grammy. Very few people even remember Buddy Deane. Just the way it should be.

It took from 1948/1949 to 1953 to move my two favorite Doris movies from first and second place down to two and three, while *Calamity Jane* took over #1 spot. I can't remember how many times I have seen this movie or how many times I have watched it either on TV or DVD…you don't want to know, but I do know some of the lines by heart if that is any indication. And if I see that it is playing anywhere on TV, I watch it. And I smile. I love this movie; it makes me feel really good. You know, heart-warming.

Naturally, I was surprised to hear that Doris had worked so hard on this movie that it caused her to have a nervous breakdown. I am certain that it was strenuous, but she still says it is her favorite of all her films, and recently, in the United Kingdom, it has been voted as the Best Movie Musical of All Time. That's right...not *Singing in the Rain* but *Calamity Jane*. The British just have class....what can I say. (And no, I have no intention of moving...I just have to continue to fight the battle to educate the folks on this side of the pond to understand that Doris is the best.)

After *Calamity Jane* cleaned up at the box office, the next film should have been another great one. Let's just say this. It may have grossed 5 million dollars at the box office, but it did not add anything to the wonderful movies that Doris had done in the past or that would come in the future. Mostly, it was a letdown. We were all anxious to see *Lucky Me* because we did not know what was in store for us.

Phil Silvers has never been a favorite of mine...not in anything. He ruined the film of *South Pacific* for me, too. I know he always thought he was funny. I didn't agree. I just found him boring. More than that, he really bothered me. I just wanted him to go away. So, whenever he was on screen with Doris, I sat there shaking my head. There could have been much better co-stars, and I felt the same way about Robert Cummings…just no real chemistry for Doris, and I think it showed. However, this film had one great scene that I just loved. That would be the sequence when Doris sang "I Speak to the Stars". It was haunting. And I will always associate that song with an event in my life.

I had reached the point in my life when it was time to have a car of my own. Mom and Dad were tired of me asking for their cars to run errands (even though 9 out of 10 times they were the ones sending me on those errands). I won't bore you with the details of my father trying to teach me how to drive. Let's just say we both made each other too nervous. So, he took me to Easy Method Driving School, and they did the job. Everything went well until I went for the actual driver's test. They took me in a car that had a clutch. I was used to driving an automatic. It did not work, and I did not pass. The second time was the charm. So I was now driving and had a license but no car. That meant "borrowing on pain of death" Mom and Dad's cars. They didn't mind sending me on errands to the store or to pick up my sisters and bring them home, but they were not anxious to lend me their cars. So.

My dad took me out shopping one day. We looked and looked and looked and settled on a 1942 blue Plymouth (I always had a thing about the color blue). After picking up the car and on the way home, I turned on the radio. And I heard, for the first time, Doris singing "I Speak to the Stars". I loved, loved, loved the song! It was a great follow-up to "Secret Love". So she was officially welcoming me to my new car. And I could not wait to buy the record and see the movie. I hate to say that although the welcome was a great one, the car was not. I can't tell you how many times I had to park the car at the top of an alley in order for it to drift into a start. It was a real lemon before the lemon laws were officially introduced. I think it lasted all of four months. And then it was time for Dad to take me shopping again. My next car was a used black Chevy (1950 vintage), and that great car not only took me through graduation from high school ,but it also took me though four years of college and another graduation. All my friends (especially those that did not have cars and did not drive) loved my good old reliable black Chevy. We often reminisce about that great car and all the good times we had in it.

There were a couple more great songs in *Lucky Me*. One was called "Love You Dearly", and the other was "Angel's Song". Neither was released. I wrote to Columbia Records several times about that, but they were adamant in their reply that "the best songs from the film, "Stars" and "Blue Bells of Broadway" were sufficient releases from that movie." Only recently did either song become available in collections…way too late. So…like *Starlift*, when Doris is on screen, this is a good movie. When she isn't, it isn't.

Earlier in this story I discussed *Young at Heart* so I won't reiterate those details. I will say, however, that I loved the on screen relationship with Doris and Gig Young. They were to appear in films together again but never as the romantic leads; how unfortunate. (The same can be said about Doris and John Gavin). Once Frank Sinatra enters the story, things change. I know (and I knew then) that a story is a story. But as a senior in high school, I just could not buy Sinatra and Day as an on-screen romantic couple. I might have changed my mind had they sung three or four songs together, but they didn't. And all my friends agreed that no one would have left Gig for Frank. It just was not believable. On their behalf, I am willing to admit that I do understand why Warner Brothers teamed Doris and Frank. At the time, they were the two hottest singing and box office stars in the country. Putting them together assured them of a box office success, and it was. And I watch it a lot...until Frank comes on to the scene. Sorry, Doris...but I honestly prefer to see you with Gig. I told her that in a letter or two, but Doris, being the lady she is, chose not to respond to that comment. After all, Frank likened her to "a convention of angels"...how could anyone fight that compliment?

One more thing, and this is a comment to the head honchos of Warner Brothers and Columbia Records at the time. They had to know this was Doris' last film for their company; she was moving on. It was a starring film for the two top singers in the U.S. at the time, and they didn't even sing any songs together. How dumb was that? Someone was surely sleeping on the job. To make matters worse, instead of using both artists on the soundtrack album (even though they sang for different labels), they each put out their own version of the songs from

Young at Heart. Doris' had the most popular of the two, but it only reached #15. An album together would have hit #1 and stayed there. Dumb!

I should also mention that there were several more outstanding songs from this movie that should have been released as singles but never were. The released songs were: "Hold Me in Your Arms" (a beautiful ballad that went nowhere and no one knows why not) with the flip side "Ready, Willing and Able" which became a Top Hit in the United Kingdom. You explain it. One of the prettiest songs ever written comes from this movie. It is called "There's A Rising Moon". It was never released. Ditto for "Till My Love Comes To Me". Yes, I have been told I should have been Doris' agent. I know one thing: I believe she would have had more top hits with me.

CHAPTER FIFTEEN:

A WHOLE NEW WORLD

1955 was a year of graduations, one for me and one, of sorts, for Doris. I graduated from high school; she graduated from Warner Brothers Studios.

For Doris, it was an amazing year. After seven years and 17 films with her home studio, she packed her things, cried a few tears, and became an independent agent. She could work for any studio, and she was in demand. The Major Home of Movie Musicals, MGM, knew a good thing when they had it, and they quickly signed Doris to star in *Love Me Or Leave Me,* the musical biography of 1920's Follies and movie star, Ruth Etting, which was released in early June and topped the box office charts all summer and into the fall. It was her only movie that year, one of the few years in which she only starred in one movie, but it was what many people consider to be the crowning glory of her entire career as a musical film star. It was an exceptional film in every way, and Doris not only sang and danced, she also acted like never before with her co-star, James Cagney, who considered her one of the very best actresses in all of Hollywood. The film grossed over 8.2 million dollars for MGM, and I am sure they were pleased. It was a box office smash, one of the biggest films of the year, and there was lots of Oscar talk. When the dust settled, it was nominated for six Oscars. It won the Best Writing Award. Cagney was nominated; Doris was not. He said at the time that if he won that award, he would give it to Doris because she truly deserved it. Since then, scores of critics have counted that as one of the biggest mistakes the Academy ever made. The soundtrack album was a phenomenal success, the biggest album of 1955, and one of the most popular albums of the entire 1950's. The big hit song from the movie, "I"ll Never Stop Loving You", was nominated for an Oscar. No…it did not win. "Love is a Many-Splendored Thing" took that nod, a difficult decision that year. The other Top 40 Song for Doris that year was called "Foolishly Yours". There was another song that year which did not chart very highly, but at my college, we liked it enough to feature it as a performance in our class show. It was called "Ooh Bang, Jiggly Jang".

Starring in *Love Me Or Leave Me* was a real career change for Doris. She was definitely not the girl next door type in this one; she was sexy, she drank, she wore revealing clothes. I am sure she was worried at the time if her fans would like the new image. I still remember the gasp in the audience when James Cagney (as Marty The Gimp) hauls off and slaps her in the face. It was no fake, either…he hauled off and hit her on the set, and her face burned for hours. And although James Garner may have cracked her ribs in a future film, I am pretty sure this is the only time in her career when she literally got slapped and did not complain because she was so much in character, as was Cagney. As for the image, it didn't matter. The movie firmly established Doris as a dramatic actress, one to be reckoned with, and that point was well brought home in her next movie in 1956. One of the most popular directors in Hollywood wanted her in his next film, and he got her.

For me, 1955 was a big year, too. I was going to start Towson State Teacher's College in the fall, and I had to get ready for some serious schooling. But first, trust me, I spent hours and hours that summer enamored with that Doris movie and writing and telling her how much I loved it. And clipping out all the articles and reviews from magazines and newspapers to put into my scrapbook. And this one was my record movie: I saw it twenty-two times. (Yes, I counted.) Since then, I have probably seen it more like a hundred times, and I never grow tired of it. Whenever I have the opportunity, I show it to others -- especially novices who have never seen it. Everyone who has seen it loves it. Although her comedies (in later years) gave her more press and more awards, this one tops the list of most of her fans as her best movie. It certainly does mine. Sometime in 1955, Doris sent me a signed still from this movie. It is the scene in which she sings "I'll Never Stop Loving You", one of my favorite scenes from the movie, and I just love it. It is one of my all-time favorite Doris songs; it expresses my feelings for Doris, too.

I was still working at the record store (almost every day by this time), but no longer working at the candy store. I was also being paid a real salary. But college was going to cost more than the stipend I was earning at Monumental Appliance. Having taken some special courses in business while in high school, I was able to apply for and got a position in both sales and office work at Towson Stationers in the heart of Towson. I loved the job, I loved the work, I loved my co-workers and my bosses (there were two). And I stayed with it throughout my years at college. The hours there and at the record store kept me in enough dollars to support me through the four years of college. I lived at home (my mother would not agree because I spent all my spare time at the college); I paid a weekly fee to my Dad for room and board (in lieu of college boarding. But I spent most of my money on gas for the car, meals at school when I was on campus, and my costly record collecting hobby.

College would have been exciting enough by itself, but by some fortunate, unplanned coincidences, I managed to be elected Freshman Class President, and that opened many new avenues for me as well. My classmates must have liked the job I did because they elected me as their leader all four years. And some of my favorite people alive (as well as some no longer) became my closest friends…the ones I did not have as a child growing up. I still see many of these folks at least once a month and others from my college class twice a year at our annual

145

reunions. We had a very close-knit class. We did lots of things together, and we established firm and long-lasting friendships.

Doris influenced me in other ways. Yes, I used to sing along to her records when I played them, and I enjoyed singing. So, when the opportunity presented itself, I joined the College Glee Club and sang with them all four years. Our director was a little old lady that everyone loved named Mrs. Weyforth. Unlike my high school teacher, I could not convert her into a Doris fan. At least… not right away. When it came out later, I sent her a copy of Doris Day's album called *You'll Never Walk Alone* (songs of faith). I am sure she loved it. Emma may have been a lot older than us, but we loved her, and she taught us a lot.

Two other guys and I (from the glee club) formed a three tenor trio. We called ourselves "The Three D's" (Don, Digger and DeVita). We sang at several college functions and really enjoyed doing that as well. Harmonizing together on Everly Brothers songs like "All I Have To Do is Dream" was a highlight of our repertoire as was old songs like "She's Got Eyes of Blue". Our glee club performed at college functions and we also recorded for Baltimore Radio Station WFBR at Christmas. We also sang at other functions such as guesting at area churches.

Each year, each class in our four year school put on an original musical assembly for the other three classes. This was my first experience at performing (thank you, Doris!). In my first show, I played a sailor seeking the hand of the daughter of King Neptune (yes, I know…). I sang the hit "Unchained Melody" as a solo, and I will never forget the applause. I was hooked! I performed in all the other shows the next four years, but I never got hooked enough to actually go out for the school dramatics club or their performances. However, this experience led, years later, to my tenure as a director of theatrical performances in four different schools and to a job I held for two years as Program Director in a summer camp in upper state New York. More on that later.

Three jobs, a steady girlfriend (which pretty much changed each year), class president, numerous activities, singing in the glee club and in a trio at various functions, working on the college newspaper, and attending classes (I never cut) were time consuming. I

147

could not live on campus (I lived within a 3-mile radius of the school), but I spent more time there than I did at home. I began the day by parking my car on a lot around 6 a.m. Then, it was off to the college switchboard (another job I held throughout college in the morning before classes began). Classes began at 8 a.m. and generally lasted till about 3 p.m. with an occasional break for a meal or to study. (Yes, I have to admit that I spent more time in the student union center than I did in the library, and that is where I learned to play pinochle.)

Freshman class meetings after regular classes, newspaper preparation and other activities filled my spare hours, along with the job at Towson Stationers whenever I had a few hours to work. (The record store job was by now Saturdays only.) Because there were so many things to do, many nights I did not get home until after 9 p.m. Most of my classmates did not know that I was a dayhop. Because I ate with the dorm students so often, they just assumed I lived in the dorms as well. Back in those days, the school was small, and it was run something like a big family. Students in all four classes did lots of things together, and the college kept us busy with film nights, speakers, dances, etc. Each class was

148

responsible for a float and other activities for Homecoming in the fall, a sponsored dance each year, an assembly in the spring and activities for May Day. That was then. Today, the school is a big university, and there are no class organizations. What a shame. Progress really is not.

So Sundays I had to catch up with church and family, not necessarily in that order, and Doris. That is when I wrote to her, entertained my little sister, waited on my father, played my records (90 percent Doris), and often played canasta with my mother and sisters. That was the case most Sundays unless there was a special event at the college. Or if I had to study for an exam (rare). I had the exams; I rarely studied, but I maintained an overall A- average and graduated in the top ten percent.

As for Doris, by this time she was a big star. So, most of her responses for these few years were on studio cards which she signed. I have to say she never neglected signing her name and that is a feat for a major star. I got many duplicates, but I scrapbooked them anyway. Hearing from Doris was always special. It still is.

CHAPTER SIXTEEN:

TWO OSCAR NODS IN 1956; MUSIC TAKES A BACKSEAT TO ACTING

More than any other year in Doris' career, 1956 was the one in which her movie star life overpowered her recording life. I don't want to give the impression that she did not record; she did, and they were some of her biggest successes, but they did take a big backseat to Doris as screen star. The movies contained at most two songs, if any; in the past, there had been anywhere from six to ten songs, and they were missed.

For the first part of 1956, Doris enjoyed musical success with one of her consistently popular albums , *Day By Day*. It was a delightful combination of great old standards from the title song through "But Not For Me", "Autumn Leaves", and the song that many fans and critics say is her best recording (me included): "I Remember You". She recorded it again years later, and it is just as beautiful. If you have not heard it, you must. It is an outstanding recording in every way, as is the entire album. This is the only Doris album that I ever wore out from playing it too much. I have three copies just in case. You know the old setting for a nice affair: soft lights, fireplace, comfy sofa, and background music? This is the music to play. You can keep Sinatra.

To go along with the new image represented by the sexy Doris from *Love Me or Leave Me*, she released a song which shocked all her fans because of its explicit nature. It was called "Let it Ring". When I would play that one for my friends, they could not believe it was Doris singing. It was, and it was great fun. She should have done that more often.

From the Broadway stage, Doris released two songs that were widely played in 1956: "Love In A Home" (from *Lil' Abner*) and "The Party's Over" (from *The Bells Are Ringing*). The latter is often used to end various shows and musical compilations.

Her first big movie of the year was directed
by one of Hollywood's most popular
directors, none other than Alfred Hitchcock.
It was a remake of his earlier 1939 film, *The
Man Who Knew Too Much.* She co-starred
in the movie with the very popular actor,
James Stewart. Doris has said of the
experience that Hitch did not give her much
direction at all. When she asked him about
it, he said, "You are doing exactly what I
want you to do."

Many critics have said that there is one 12-
minute sequence featuring Doris (when she
does not say a single word) that should have
won her an Oscar nomination. It took place
in the Royal Albert Hall in London and she
does the entire sequence with face and body
expressions which end in a piercing scream.
Another sequence has her going through an
emotional breakdown. Both are excellent
examples of acting, but no Oscar nod. There
was one for the best song in a film. It won
the Oscar and has become Doris Day's
signature song. Of course, I mean "Que
Sera, Sera". Funny story here. When she
went to the studio to record this song for
release, she commented on the way out,
"That's the last time you'll ever hear that
song". And the rest is history. It is the one
song by which she is known today if people

remember at all that she was a singer! I hate to say how many people have said to me "Who is Doris Day?" when I bring up her name. If I mention the song, 80 percent know who I mean. If they don't, they then get treated to my Doris Day sermon! With the exception of that song, there was one other in the film. It was a beautiful ballad called "We'll Love Again". That is the one that no one ever heard again, even though it was one of Doris' favorites and she recorded it again on another album.

I said in the chapter title that there were two Oscar nods, and there were. The title of her next film from 1956 was also nominated for Best Song in a Film. It was called "Julie", and the film co-starred Louis Jordan. Doris spends the entire film running from a jealous husband trying to kill her, another of those films shot in black and white which should have been in color, especially with all the beautiful location shots from Carmel, California (the place Doris calls home today). I have some beautiful signed still shots from this movie which Doris sent to me that year. Doris and Louis Jordan made a handsome couple, and the same is true of Doris with James Stewart. She was finally being teamed with reasonable , believable and popular co-stars.

The summer of 1956 was the last summer I spent at home in Baltimore. That was also the summer that my parents went to Florida for a week or two and Mom from Allentown came to visit, along with Anna Marie and Helen. It was a delightful vacation during vacation; their company was always a good thing. And with Mom fixing all the meals, we ate like kings and queens. The four of us went twice to see *The Man Who Knew*. It was not like the good old musicals, but we still enjoyed it and wished Doris would have sung more songs. Still, some Doris singing is always better than no songs at all.

CHAPTER SEVENTEEN:

HOLLYWOOD TO BROADWAY FOR DORIS; MIKE BECOMES A DIFFERENT KIND OF LEADER

I said at the outset of writing this memoir that it would not be necessarily purely chronological in nature, and yet it seems to be going in that direction. I will be skipping large sections of years and combining some as we move ahead but, for now, the yearly chronology works.

1957 was the year in which Hollywood decided to film the hit Broadway musical, *The Pajama Game.* The producers brought the entire cast of the show to the screen except for the part of Babe Williamson. That was the part played by Doris, replacing Janis Paige. (She had been Doris' co-star in her first movie, and she would star with her again in the future so there were no hard feelings between them about this part.) The movie was to gross 5 million dollars, and the soundtrack album reached the Top Ten. The two great song sequences from the film were: "I'm Not At All in Love" (sung by Doris with the entire female cast) and "There Once Was A Man/Woman" (a duet between Doris and co-star John Raitt). It was a fun movie, and it was wonderful to see Doris back in a movie musical. About this film, critics have said it is one of the best transformations from stage show to movie musical ever done. It was another year in which Doris only did one movie, but she released two albums. Besides the great soundtrack from the movie, the second was kind of a sequel to *Day By Day*. This time it was called *Day By Night*, a sensuous, lush collection of songs that developed the night theme, including: "Close Your Eyes", "Moonglow" and "The Night We Called It A Day". Talk about soft and sexy!

As a sophomore in college, I was having my first experience with teaching. Fortunately, the college made us participate in several teaching experiences before we graduated. Just think how awful it would be if one prepared for four years to be a teacher and then actually hated it once on the job! My first experience was in elementary school - long enough to tell me I wasn't the type to teach little children. They have to be told EVERYTHING. So, my second experience was with 7th graders and I loved that. And I thought I was ready; I had had enough college prep. I wanted to start, but I still had two years of school to go.

Something else occurred for me this year, and it was another new experience for me. Several of my friends and I decided to try becoming YMCA camp counselors for the summer. It was good pay, but it meant we would be away for almost the entire summer. The college guidance department said it would be good experience for future teachers. So I took a leave of absence from all my jobs, and it was a counselor I became at Camp Conoy in Lusby, Maryland, about a 4-hour drive from my house.

We signed on for an eight-week stint (with very good pay, which we received in a lump sum at the end of the camp assignment). We didn't need any money; they paid all our expenses while we were there. We got three days off between the two four-week sessions, and we drove home to get caught up a bit with family life before continuing another four-week stint.

Each of us as a counselor was assigned to a cabin group of 8 boys, and they were our charges day and night. I had a cabin of 6th graders, and they kept me jumping, but were a lot of fun. We were on a first name basis with the kids; no formality. That would cause a bit of a problem the following year when I did my next practice teaching experience. Several of my campers were in my class, and they wanted to call me "Mike" instead of "Mr. DeVita". I didn't mind but my supervising teacher did not consider it respectful. So, we were formal in the classroom but still good friends outside.

There was no time for letter writing or corresponding or whatever; the kids were a total responsibility. I missed my music and my letters to Doris, but I am sure she understood. By the time we tucked the kids in at night, we were pooped and ready for bed ourselves. It was definitely a really worthwhile experience and one I would never trade. It was to be the first year of many for me and one of my all-time best friends, even to this day, Dave King.

That was also the year that I established the policy of waking up each day at 5 a.m. to be on the job by 6 a.m. I never lost that habit until years after I retired. When I started teaching, I sometimes had to wake up the custodians in order to get into the building early. I got a lot accomplished before the rest of the staff arrived for the day. Today, I still get up early (around 6). Instead of going to a job, I either go the gym (I should go more) or start working on the website and other assorted jobs. I rarely eat breakfast that early though…more like 9:30 a.m. and skip lunch. I am one of those who gain weight just looking at food. (I recently joined Weight Watchers and do what most do…lose, gain and lose, gain. And I regretfully add that, unfortunately, I am not like Doris in that respect. She is, has been and will always be thin. Lucky her!)

Side note: When Marty (Doris' husband) died, Doris discovered that, due to some bad business decisions by others, she was penniless and in debt. Luckily, Terry was able to work it out along with the courts and restore at least some of the money that she had lost. These same decision-makers also squelched too many things that should have been career-boosters for Doris, especially the starring role as Nellie Forbush in *South Pacific*. And they were too quick to sign her to deals without telling her. Her son would have been a much better manager. Things

161

should have been much different, and she should have been an even bigger star than she ended up being, especially with her music. What a shame. Fortunately, she has scads of loyal fans that love her in anything and love all her music and are with her to this day.

Another side note:

It is now almost Christmas (mid-December, 2011), and I am still writing. I said I would let you know when it happened. My totally refurbished scrapbooks have arrived, and they are beautiful. Carol is a genius. They did not lose their feel of antiquity; they have just become more of a treasure trove. Now they can be read, and they don't fall apart. All of the magazines are in one bound book, and the scrapbooks now number three (the third one having some empty pages for all the notes and letters I still hope to get from my "secret love").

*The years 2011 and early 2012 are something quite remarkable for fans of Doris Day, old and new. The powers that be talked her into releasing a new album!!! It is comprised of material mostly recorded in the 1980's, engineered by son Terry while Doris was doing the **Best Friends** cable*

*show in 1986. The recordings were never
released. Some modern geniuses took the
raw recordings, added some great new
instrumental music and voila! Doris ended
up with a Top Ten Record once again. As I
write these words (Jan 8, 2012), it is still the
#1 album in best sellers on Amazon in Jazz
and Vocal Jazz Categories and is still
making a showing in the Pop, Vocal Pop
and Broadway and Vocalists as well. It goes
up and down on the lists because Amazon
gives an hourly update each day. (Amazon
just happens to be the largest seller of
recorded music worldwide). This is quite a
coup for Doris. She is the oldest female
singing star to ever have a recording of new
material in the Top Ten. This feat was also
accomplished when it was released earlier
in the UK, and it is a big seller currently
worldwide. (In all fairness, Tony Bennett
has been vying with her on the charts. He is
no spring chicken either, but he is younger
than Doris by a few years.) I couldn't save
this great news for later…had to include it
now. Yes!!!*

CHAPTER EIGHTEEN:

1958 - DORIS HITS HIGH GEAR; MIKE'S FUTURE CAREER STARTS IN EARNEST

The next year was like a total whirlwind of frenetic activity for both Doris Day and me. For Doris, it was more of some of the most important movies in her entire career, which lead to the only time that she garnered an Academy Award Nomination. For the next few years, she would continue to be "World Favorite Movie Star" and "Biggest Box Office Draw" (a title she maintains today.) No one has ever surpassed her title as Biggest Female Box Office Draw of All Time. Check these links on your computer:

http://www.quigleypublishing.com/MPalmanac/Top10/Top10_lists.html
http://www.dorisday.net/box-office.html

Doris got to star with the admitted King of Hollywood, Clark Gable, in *Teacher's Pet*, a very successful film in 1958 which grossed $5,800,000. (That one far outdistanced the other movie she did that year, *Tunnel of Love*, even though the latter still grossed three and half million dollars.) Doris was even nominated for a Golden Globe for Best Actress in a Comedy. There have been all kinds of comments made as to why it was not as successful as *Pet*. My take on it is that Richard Widmark, first off, is no Clark Gable, and he was trying to do comedy, which was definitely not his forte'. Doris far outshone him in that respect, and Gig Young could not save this one. Perhaps if Gig had played the husband, that might have worked better (remember the great screen chemistry Doris had with him in *Young At Heart*, and he had also just appeared with her in *Teacher's Pet*). I also wonder if the movie had been filmed a year later with Rock Hudson and Tony Randall in the leads if that would have made a difference…but that is only conjecture. Doris, Rock and Tony as a team were yet to come.

Personally, I liked both movies and at the same time was also disappointed in them. Remember, I am a true Doris fan. If she is in a movie, then it is going to be a good movie regardless. (Yes, there was one much later that was not on a list of my favorites, but if it was Doris, I would see it and love it.) Warner's was saving money again and did movies in black and white. I suppose it is excusable for *Teacher's Pet* because the movie is about the often black and white newspaper business, but for *Tunnel* there was no excuse. Also, as a young man at the age of 21, I could definitely not fathom Clark Gable as a costar for Doris. He looked old enough to be her father. (But, Clark was Clark and the combination took in a lot of dollars!) As for Widmark, I think Doris enjoyed working with him. She has said that he was a lot of fun and that they got along very well. That chemistry did not come across on the big screen. And in 1958, even the majority of television shows were doing brilliant color so producing anything in black and white would not compete very well, would it? Corporate bean counters then and now have never been noted for common sense or for much of anything, for that matter. Some people just never learn.

For me, 1958 was almost a blur. It was my junior year in College. I was engaged to a girl I should have married (she might have kept me sane.) I was Class President once again and the junior year was one of the busiest times for class activities, and the graduating Class of 1959 was a very active group. I started the very time-consuming classes in the block of programs required for future teachers (a two-year series of very specialized classes in our major, which was, of course, education). These classes took away a lot of free time and involved many homework hours. I started the pre-teaching activities before actual student teaching the next year and had practice experiences in both 7th and 8th grade (and loved them both) and one with 6th graders (too young) as well. By doing these I occasionally had to miss a class or two, and that did not make me happy. (I hated to miss classes…I know, very unusual… even abnormal!)

Regardless of the blur of activity, I made time for Doris whenever a movie came out and always talked my friends into seeing the films with me. Like I said before, they tolerated Doris because of me even if some of them were not fans.

Musically, Doris had several minor hits in 1958 and one gigantic one. Of course, as was still the case, the title songs for the movies were pushed, and they both appeared in the Top 40; the more popular one was "Teacher's Pet", but I liked "Tunnel of

Love" better because it was a great jitterbug tune. The other minor hit was Doris' take on a song from the movie *Marjorie Morningstar*. The song was called "A Very Precious Love", a beautiful ballad, which was nominated for an Academy Award that year. No, it did not win.

On the album scene, Columbia released two albums that year, and one was a big mistake (the way I see it.) Early in the year, Columbia decided it needed to make a few more bucks on their highest paid and highest grossing recording star at the time. So instead of releasing a new album, they collected what they considered to be all of Doris' hits up to that time and released an album called *Doris Day's Greatest Hits*, one of her consistent bestselling albums today. The first track on the album was the newest single release, a monster hit for Doris that year, called "Everybody Loves a Lover". Why was it a mistake? Because that was the last Top Ten single hit that Doris ever had. I would have preferred they wait another ten years and produce a two-disc album with greatest hits rather than put one out with only twelve songs. In a sense, producing this album in 1958 became prophetic because Doris had no other great hits after that, at least not in the US. (She managed to crack the Top 100 a few times after that, but never again did she hit the Top Ten. That is, until 2011 with her album, *My Heart*.) I should point out that in 1958, recording companies had not yet started to release Greatest Hit Series in *several* volumes. It was just a one shot deal per artist then.

"Lover" became one of my all-time Doris favorites for lots of reasons, mostly because it was infectious. I loved the beat, I loved the way she dueted with herself, and everyone else liked it, too. It was neck and neck that spring and summer with Peggy Lee's recording of "Fever". A lot of the deejays would play them back to back on the radio, and both were popular on the nation's jukeboxes. (I recently saw a jukebox in a nearby diner, and that song is still on their jukebox!) At college, we decorated for our Junior Class Prom while listening to the two songs over and over on the record player. We had stacks of 45's, but each time some of the songs were shifted for new ones, both of these remained in the queue. And I can honestly say I was not the one who kept putting them back on! I was accused, but honest, it wasn't me.

Toward the end of October, and in time for Christmas buying, Columbia distributed the only two-lp release ever done by Doris (before 2012), her tribute to the movies called "*Hooray for Hollywood*". The album contained 24 songs by Doris…what a feast for her fans, and what a feast the recording was as well. Unfortunately, this collection is no longer available today in the same two-lp format in which it was released. Some of the songs are available in a single volume, but today's buyers are missing the richness of the original set. This was the quote from the liner of the original album:

> *"In selecting the twenty-four songs for this collection,Doris Day has aimed at a cross-section of some of the most memorable; some from almost-forgotten films, some from dramatic movies, some among the most popular songs of all time. In design, the collection is a kind if impressionistic souvenir of great songs from the movies, a salute to brilliant craftsmen and the magic that is Hollywood at its best by one of Hollywood's most versatile and accomplished artists."*

I remember this album all too well; I heard it for the first time on my only driving trip to South Carolina over Thanksgiving Vacation that year…I went with a friend from camp to visit his Southern family, and we previewed the album all the way down and all the way back. I keep telling you my friends are very tolerant of my enthusiasm for Doris.

"Hooray for Hollywood" ranks up there among Doris' very best album collections. Many of the songs she selected are ones that are still played on easy listening themed stations today whenever a Doris recording is aired. My special favorites included these: "Cheek To Cheek", "It's Easy To Remember", "I'll Remember April", a gutsy version of "Blues in the Night", one that Judy Garland asked her to record…"Over the Rainbow", "Nice Work If You Can Get It", "In The Still of the Night" and a great new version of "Three Coins in the Fountain" complete with a host of violins. There were 24 songs and all of them really terrific. My friend and I disagreed all the way down and back about which were the best cuts, and we changed our minds constantly. Less I forget, I should add that Doris' version of the title song is considered by many to be the best ever interpretation of that wonderful paean to Hollywood.

Summer time came. Dave King (whom I mentioned earlier) and I had decided to investigate jobs at a different summer camp, this time in upper state New York in the heart of the Catskill Mountains. Our former camp had closed. This new camp, opening its doors for the first time, sounded like a dream come true. When we arrived for the first week of orientation before the camp actually brought in the campers, we had to help with final construction on some of the cabins which were not yet finished. There I was on a roof hammering nails, mostly at a crooked angle. A builder I was not. I mean, for heaven's sake, I even had trouble when I tried hammering nails straight…but it didn't matter, there I was helping to get the camp ready and feeling good about it, too. I never became adept at hammering or tinkering, but some parts of me are still there on those cabin roofs.

In our previous camp experience, the living spaces were in dinky little cabins, all of us in one room, with outside cold water showers and outhouses as bathrooms (sometimes equipped with copperhead snakes on the floor). In the new camp, our cabins were each equipped with a real bathroom and

173

showers in a separate room with a closing door, a private room for the counselors with a closing door, a major room with eight built-in bunks for the campers, and a real working fireplace. (Yes, it got cold at night and in the early summer mornings in the Catskills.)

When hired, with only one year of previous experience (and I guess because of our ages as well as our college majors), we became Village Chiefs instead of just ordinary cabin counselors. We each had our own cabin of campers, but we also were responsible for coordinating and administering four other cabin groups and the counselors in what was called a little Village of five cabin groups. So we kind of directed the activities for about 50 people each. Dave was attached to the older campers (age 14 and up). He was well over 6 feet tall. I was with the 2nd level campers (ages 11, 12 and 13). I was only 5'4" tall. The camp had five over-all villages and a group that was more out of camp than in. I guess the name that would most closely be associated with the kind of job we had would be Administrative Assistant/Program Director and Unit Supervisor.

The camp was absolutely beautiful and sprawling over many acres complete with waterfalls and a man-made lake. The local Sunday magazine section in one New Jersey newspaper did a feature on the camp, which they titled "Plush Playground For Youth". Compared to our previous camp, it was plush indeed. We stayed for eight weeks and even got to go to New York City and see some plays on our days off (a 4-hour ride and we had two and a half days off every two weeks.) We also got a night off once every two weeks, and we then often motored into close-by Liberty, New York for dinner and a movie. (Liberty is famous for being located in what was known at the time as the "Borscht Belt" and often had famous movie stars ensconced at the local Brown's Hotel.) Today, the entire area is owned by The Frost Valley Association.

We both loved the experience. I continued going back in the summers for the next eight years. (Dave and his wife Shirley are still actively connected to the camp today). That experience undoubtedly helped me to become the organized and competent teacher that I was for 33 years. Eventually I became the Camp Program Director, and Dave was the Camp Director. Today, Dave is one of the major alumni. At the time it was known as YMCA Camp Wawayanda. It is better known in New Jersey and upper state New York as the Frost Valley Association. It has mushroomed quite considerably from its earlier beginnings when we helped to open it in 1959. (Check out the website: www.frostvalley.org.)

Dave and I both loved it because of the Christian spirit it instilled in everyone who worked there and everyone who played there. Helping each other was a big theme and a lesson that could not hurt a few modern kids. I was lucky to have that rich experience; it taught me many things about how to get along with other people, as well as how to be a leader (even more than the one I was learning by being Class President at College for four years). Both experiences helped me greatly in my teaching career. And being a fan of Doris Day did not hurt; she was a wonderful role model of the kind of person I wanted to be.

CHAPTER NINETEEN:

AN OSCAR NOMINATION AND A DIPLOMA

1959 was a pivotal year, in many ways, for both Doris and me. In her case, it was to be the year in which she received her first and only Academy Award Nomination for Best Actress. After the disappointing previous film (*It Happened To Jane*), *Pillow Talk* would become a box office smash, grossing 18.7 million dollars and would team, for the first of three times, Doris with Rock Hudson (what has become the top standard in films for a top romantic comedy team). And Mr. Second Banana, Tony Randall, was no small part of the casting. Much has been written about this film and about all of its awards; it won almost everything except the Oscar for Best Film! (It did win 4 Oscars for writing, story and screenplay, and garnered 6 other nominations.) Its other awards included:

177

GOLDEN GLOBES:

Best Actress/ Best Supporting Actor
Best Motion Picture-Comedy

LAUREL AWARDS:

Top Comedy
Top Female Performance   (Doris)
Top Male Performance (Rock)

And there were others. Much has also been
written about the fact that the Oscar is rarely
awarded to a comedy. Those who have
starred in, directed or produced a comedy
know for certain that it is the most difficult
of all kinds of acting. One can rarely be
taught comic timing; it is in-bred; you just
have to have the knack. Doris had it and
more so in this and other comedy films that
would follow (especially *Lover, Come Back,
That Touch of Mink, The Thrill of it All,* and
Move Over, Darling.)

As usual, the Academy continued to ignore
Doris and her great skills. It really makes me
mad. I am sure it didn't faze her very much.
I am almost certain she was disappointed
when she did not win, but Miss Good Sport
never showed it. As she indicated in a letter
to me that year (and elsewhere in print), she

never expected to win an Academy Award. She says she was given a job, and she did it to the best of her ability and felt good about it, as she most certainly should have. She was glad her fans liked it. She didn't need the icing on the cake, but her fans thought differently, and they still do. We want her to have the cake *and the icing*.

This film did more for Doris than she may have realized at the time, but it did not go unnoticed by her critics in print. Instead of that sweet girl next door, she became a sexy, sophisticated and liberated woman, a role model for those young ladies just starting their own careers in what was, at the time, mostly a man's world…certainly no longer the case. And her clothes took on a complete fashion overhaul…she literally became a model on screen with clothes to die for. That continued through most of her films from then on and picked up in the 1970's on *The Doris Day Show* on television where she included in many episodes actual fashion shows. There were also hundreds of magazine spreads at the time when she appeared one year later in *Midnight Lace*. The movie was scary, a thriller…the clothes were talked about all over the place.

On the music scene in 1959, Doris took us on a special trip to the land of light swing with an album called *Cuttin' Capers*. Besides the lively title song, there were some really good takes on some great standards, including: "Makin' Whoopee", "I'm Sitting on Top of the World", "Steppin' Out With My Baby" (which could have been a great follow-up single to "Everybody Loves A Lover" if it had been released), "Fit As A Fiddle", and a wonderfully sexy arrangement (to go right along with the newly-discovered Sexy Doris) of "Why Don't We Do This More Often."

This was also the year when Doris moved from the Top Ten Biggest Grossing Box Office Stars to Number One. She remained in that position longer than any other female star in movie history and continues to hold that record today. Like I said, 1959 was certainly a pivotal year for her, and now everyone took even more note of this great star…worldwide. Fun loving, Good Neighbor, Girl Next Door became Doris Day, Legend, right where her status is today.

Personally, 1959 was a hectic year. As Senior Class President, I had hundreds of jobs that had to be completed in preparation for graduation. In addition, this was the year for major student teaching experiences: we had to be in the classroom for two 9-week experiences of mostly supervised teaching. That meant arriving at our assigned school before 7 a.m. every day and staying until the school day closed (around 3:30), in addition to supervising any extra-curricular or after school duties to which our cooperating teachers were assigned. I experienced homeroom duties, the attendance register, keeping a current grade book updated on a daily basis, after school detention, lunch duty, chaperone school activities like dances and athletic events, attending faculty meetings, etc. etc. Then, it was go home and get started on grading papers and planning for the next day's lessons. It was a difficult responsibility to get all the required jobs done, and to this day, I honestly do not know how I managed all the responsibilities that were inherent in the job of an English Teacher in Junior High School. That said, you will remember that besides that I also had responsibilities at the college connected to my role as Class President, as well as my jobs on the student newspaper and the All College Council. And I was still working several hours a week at Towson Stationers in various capacities from sales clerk to stock work to assistant secretary. I did that job throughout the four years of college, and I still worked part time at the record store on Saturdays. I had to make special, careful arrangements with two of my best friends, Bob Mayr, who was Class Vice President and his soon-to-be wife, Ruth, who was Class Treasurer. I had introduced them as freshmen, and they were an item throughout college, as were my friends Dave King and his wife, Shirley. While I was out student teaching, they were at the college to handle some of the class duties, and vice versa. Obviously, we could not all be in both places at the same time, no matter what the writers say about living in things called parallel universes!

I do not want to leave the impression that I did not like student teaching....I loved it! First off, I had requested the school from which I graduated when I was in junior high school, and I was lucky enough to get it. And yes, there were teachers on the faculty at the time who had been teachers of mine when I was a student. It was great to be in the same boat as them this time, and they were nothing if not welcoming. They were glad to see me and helped as much as they could. And I managed to catch the smile I got when I came in the faculty room. I think they were glad to see a former student become one of the pack!

From the first day I set foot in the classroom (my first experience was with 7th Graders), I knew I was going to love being a teacher. Generally, student teachers observe for a few weeks, then they gradually take on the teacher's full load before the experience is over. I observed for two days. My direct supervising teacher (Mrs. Elsie Street) had me teaching on Day 3, and I had one half of her full load the beginning of the next week. The fact that she was a strict (but highly respected) teacher made me go the same route, and I never regretted that. I was strict but I was fair, and the students reacted well to that. It took them a week to get used to me every year, but after the first week, we got along famously. I got along well with a good 97 percent. There will always be that 3 percent no matter how hard you try.

After the first nine weeks, I was back at college for a block of required courses called "Teaching in Junior High School". The irony of that is explicit in the title…I had just finished doing nine weeks of in school teaching. Now, being in a classroom where we were learning how to teach was a bit strange, not to mention mostly redundant.

It was good to be back at the college for a couple reasons as I intimated earlier…there were lots of projects to accomplish inherent in the job of a Class President helping his peers to get ready for graduation. In addition, at this point, I was engaged to be married to a sweet girl named Gretchen, who was feeling a bit neglected (and rightly so). And there was another girl in my life being neglected as well….I refer to Doris. I did not have time to breathe, much less to correspond. So this gave me the opportunity to catch up…although Doris was in such a whirlwind of success this year that I am sure she probably never noticed.

The nine weeks flew by, and it was time for my second student teaching experience, this time in a different school. We were not allowed to return to either the same school or the same kind of situation. This time around, I was placed in a school in a slightly less affluent neighborhood, where the students were not as well off as they were in my previous school, and they were a year older…the "dreaded 8th Graders", as they were often referred to. They also were not as easy to win over as the others had been. Because it was my second experience, my cooperating/supervising teacher (Mr. Robert Huber) felt that we should start in the classroom as quickly as possible. I was teaching before the end of the 2nd day. Once again, I loved it...the school, the students, the faculty were all just great. It was just as demanding as the first experience, and I was having just as much fun. In addition, I was becoming friends with my cooperating teacher (so much so that when school was out in June, he talked me into joining him and another friend on a cruise to the Island of Bermuda...a trip I will always remember as one of my favorites.) Explaining that one to my fiancée was not an easy task, and especially when she realized that by the end of June, I would be back at camp in upper state New York once again for the majority of the summer. That probably was the straw that broke the camel's back because by the end of August, the engagement was off. Again, not a bad thing considering the fact that come September 1, I would be starting a career that demanded the major part of every day and most nights. I have heard it said that "truly good teachers are married to the job". I understand that well. Most of my friends understand that, too. I can't tell you how many times I heard: "you have to do some things for yourself, too, once in a while". That admonition mostly fell on deaf ears...my students and that job always came first.

Meanwhile, back at college for the last few weeks before the end of May, 1959, time flew and I was preparing my class and myself for graduation. We had the usual Class responsibilities: the original show performance produced by the seniors for the rest of the school (a problem because so many students were out teaching and did not have time to participate), the homecoming float, May Day Activities, Senior Prom, Graduation Ceremonies and all those things that lead up to it, etc. etc. At my ripe old age today, I could not fathom doing all that and still being able to breathe. At the age of 20 or 21, though, we seemed invincible. And so, we got through it. And we graduated the first week in June, and then a crowd of us took off for Ocean City, Maryland for a chaperoned week in the sun and surf, after which I came home in enough time for the cruise mentioned above. Right after that, it was off to Camp Wawayanda for the rest of the summer.

But 1959 was not over yet…it was also the year in which I started the career I would embrace for 33 years, that of an English Teacher. September came and I began. I often wrote to Doris about my experiences as a teacher, and she seemed to get a kick out of my letters…at least, she intimated as much. I will share some of those funny experiences as we move along and as they are pertinent to my story.

You may recall that my experiences with student teaching had been in grades 7 and 8 where the students, for the most part, were about my size (I was 5'4"). My very first teaching assignment was in Grade 9 (where most of the students towered well over me.) Of course, the usual fears set in…would they walk all over me? Would they like me? Could I handle them? I needn't have worried. Mrs. Street and Mr. Huber had done their jobs well. They taught me how to take over from day 1 and stay in charge all the way through, strictly at first and then gradually easing up, until there is a good working relationship between student and teacher. That lesson stood me well for all my teaching years, and helped me even more when I started directing musical productions (like *Hello Dolly!* and *Fiddler On The Roof*) that involved close to 200 students together in one place at one time needing explicit direction. They also needed what most students really need…lots of encouragement, which I always tried to supply.

I will not bore you with 33 years' worth of teaching experiences because the book would go on forever…besides, this story is about my relationship with Doris. And to that I now return. And so much for my earlier comments about not telling the story in chronological order...that seems to be the course the book has taken thus far.

Another brief side note:

I really expected to have this book finished by now. It is currently mid-February 2012, and I am not even halfway through my journey. I hope you are enjoying it so far. Something else has distracted my efforts for a few months. Briefly stated, there were (in no special order): a computer crash that forced the expense of a new computer and weeks of getting things back to normal, the annual holidays (both Thanksgiving and Christmas) and all that is implied by them, and the preparation for my trip to California, from which I just returned. About that, I have both good news and bad news.

The bad news is that although I was in Carmel/Monterey, I was not able to convince Doris to let me visit. I would love to have taken her out to dinner or whatever, but that was not to be. (I was in touch with her business manager as well as her best friend, and I was assured that I would receive a call because Doris was currently seeing no one.) And that phone call is the subject of both good and bad news.

I was on a Trafalgar Tour, and if you have ever been on one of these excursions, you must realize they do not leave you with much time to yourself. The evening of our arrival in Monterey, I received a phone call from Doris' friend Nancy who was calling for Doris. The bad news is that I missed it!! The call was placed as we were departing from the bus and gathering luggage on our way to the hotel rooms, and it was so noisy, I never heard the phone ring!!! When I arrived in the room and checked the phone, I found the call had been made. The message was that Nancy was calling for Doris and was sorry I was not able to answer the phone. She said she would call back later that night or the next day. Neither of those things happened. I assumed they would call the next day, when we were staying in Yosemite National Park. That was until we were informed on the bus that morning that there would be no cell phone service in Yosemite. I quickly got on my cell phone and made a call to Doris' manager and informed him of that fact before I totally lost service.

I then called my friend Carol in Georgia, who has recently visited Doris twice and who is also friendly with Doris' friend, Nancy. With her intercession and to make a long story short, I was told to enjoy the rest of my tour and that the phone call would be made once I got home, probably on Monday (which is today)…and I am anxiously sitting by my phone!

I will add here that I loved the trip to Sunny California (from San Diego all the way to San Francisco), but most of all, I truly loved Hollywood (which I have never seen before). I was able to see and take pictures of the two stars Doris has on the Hollywood Walk of Fame, as well as the name and prints in cement at Grauman's Theatre. Our tour guide had met Doris several times and he kept telling me how wonderful she is (he did not need to tell me that; I already knew it.) The other thing I loved was the short visit to Carmel late the next day. I was able to rush to The Cyprus Inn (the hotel which Doris co-owns.) I took lots of pictures and talked with many of the personnel at the hotel who regaled me with stories of Doris and her pet-friendly Inn. (They also told me that they rarely see her at the hotel anymore; her visits are few and very far between.) That is so sad.

I could easily see why Doris fell in love with the area. It is a beautiful seaside resort on the Pacific where the waves come crashing against the rocks and sand. We were not able to visit her house; few people knew where it was and our bus driver was not inclined to drive the route of Carmel Valley Drive to The Loft overlooking the golf course at Quail Lodge, which is about as much as I know regarding its location. Actually, I would never impose on Doris in that way. I respect her privacy and would never jeopardize our years' long relationship by causing her any kind of problem. I would love to have given her a big hug and thanked her for all the joy she supplied to my life, but I suspect she is well aware of that by now. She can visit my website any time she wishes (www.sampod4u.com) and see how much she is respected and loved. She has my address and phone number, and they are always readily available to her. Keep your fingers crossed that the call is made and I will let you know in these pages when it happens.

CHAPTER TWENTY:

ANOTHER MISSED OSCAR NOD

In 1960, Doris appeared in two really good films. The first paired her with the unlikely leading man, David Niven. I found that combination a bit strange, but it worked and became one of the most popular films of the year, *Please Don't Eat The Daisies*. It was based on Jean Kerr's popular book of the same title and grossed over 11 million dollars. It was also very instrumental in beginning her reign as Hollywood's #1 Female Box Office Star, a reign that no female star has ever surpassed, even through today. She was in the Top Ten for most of her career and #1 for four years in a row. Something else about "Daisies": one of the co-stars was Janis Paige (who had starred with Doris in Doris' first movie and the one who Doris replaced in the film version of *The Pajama Game*). In 2010, when I was doing a radio show on the internet, Janis Paige was one of those who called in to wish Doris a Happy Birthday the day we were having a special birthday celebration for Doris. So, obviously Janis has remained friendly with Doris all those years, and there were no hard feelings when she was replaced in *The Pajama Game.*

And then came *Midnight Lace.* It was a movie that certainly should have garnered Doris another Oscar nomination, but such was not the case. In one scene, she totally fell apart: it was a complete nervous breakdown on the screen and a remarkable performance for someone known primarily for comedies and musicals. This must have been her year for starring with Brits. First, David Niven and now Rex Harrison and Roddy McDowall. In smaller parts, the film also featured Myrna Loy (in somewhat of a comeback role) and John Gavin, one of Hollywood's Handsomest Actors. He and Doris should have been teamed in many future films. They never were. They were beautiful together.

Musically, Doris released three albums in 1960. The first was somewhat of a departure for Doris, an interesting concept album in which she gave some very informative advice to the ladies. It was called *What Every Girl Should Know.* Songs like "What Does A Woman Do", "Not Only Should You Love Him", "You Can't Have Everything" and "A Fellow Needs A Girl" aptly expressed the theme. But the album also contained other gems like: "When You're Smiling", "Mood Indigo" and "Something Wonderful."

The other (and more successful album in sales that year) was titled *Show Time*. It was the only album ever released by Doris in which she sang songs from popular Broadway shows, and it even contained an intro and finale of a song written expressly for the album called "Show Time". The album is a wonderful collection of Broadway show tunes and should have been the first of many albums in that vogue. It featured songs from the most popular Broadway Shows of all time, including: *South Pacific*, *My Fair Lady*, *Oklahoma* and *Carousel*. Her recording of "The Sound of Music" went on to win a Grammy nod as the Best Performance by a Female Vocalist, even when recordings of the song from the original casts were available!

The third album reached The Top 30 in best-selling albums and was called *Listen To Day*. This time around, Columbia was looking for a way to cash in on the singles that Doris had released since her Greatest Hits album in 1958 and add a few more songs to flush it out so that fans would buy it for the new songs. They got that one right.

Single hits from 1959 through 1960 were included in the album: "Pillow Talk", "Anyway The Wind Blows", "Love Me in the Daytime", "I Enjoy Being A Girl", and "Tunnel of Love". A few flip sides from those records were thrown in along with two songs never before released: "Oh! What A Lover You'll Be" and "No". Fans loved it and so did the record-buying public who placed it in the Top 30. Me? I bought it, of course. I bought anything by Doris back then, and I still do (hundreds of collections which I already own in other sources). Fans do that. As for the new material, I think "No" could have been a big hit, but it was never released. Columbia Records… holding the bag, once again.

I can't tell you how many times I have played these albums. They contain some of my favorite Doris songs. I love "A Fellow Needs a Girl", and Doris' interpretation of "A Wonderful Guy" shows immediately why she should have starred in the film version of *South Pacific*. The role could have been written for her! I think she was offered the part, but her agent was asking for too much money (and Mitzi Gaynor was willing to do it for next to nothing). As a result, the finished product ended up being a mediocre filming of a Broadway show that could have been a real treasure had it starred Doris.

I wrote to Doris several times that year both about both the movies and the albums because I loved them so much, and she was humbly grateful in her responses as always. When I started directing Broadway musicals in high school in the 80's and we did *South Pacific*, I had the female leads listen to Doris' version of "A Wonderful Guy" to try to model their singing in that way. And it worked…we had sold out performances both nights. (High schools usually only did a show for two nights; it was too expensive to do any more.) And yes, it was one whale of a lot of work for only two nights, but we did it year after year after year without a second thought.

The biggest problem was keeping the kids up so that the second night was as good as the first! (It usually was! As a director, I did something that would help that issue. I then began double casting key roles so that the audiences would want to see the show with different performers and come for both nights.) That idea was not popular with the student actors, but it made both of them better in each performance, knowing there was competition. (And in a few instances, it saved us when one of our leads got sick and could not perform!) It was a charmer for ticket sales, as well.

For me, from 1959 through 1966, I was teaching 9th Grade Core. For those who never heard of that, it was a combination of two subjects (English and Social Studies). Because there were so many different subjects involved in that combination (Literature, Grammar, Speech, etc. on one side/History, Geography, Current Events, etc. on the other), we were assigned two classes and had them each for three periods a day in a seven period day. The object was to correlate the two subjects: for example, if studying a certain phase of history, we could correlate by reading and writing about that in the English portion of the subject. Personally, I found it to be an excellent way of tying social studies and English together, especially in literature and composition. The problem was that too few teachers were adequately trained in both subjects. As a result, student experiences were uneven if they had a teacher who stressed history and not English and vice versa.

By the time 1966 rolled around, I was teaching just English and now had five classes a day, along with one planning period and one period of assigned duties. Such was the role of a junior high teacher in the sixties in Baltimore County. In addition, I was doing the school newspaper and am fortunate that I had such wonderful students to help produce a paper of which we were all proud. It was professionally printed (thanks to our school PTA Association) and came out every month. My students and I spent many hours after school putting it together, but I have to admit I really much preferred the job of directing shows to newspaper sponsor. On the other hand, it afforded us the opportunity to feature prominent articles on the features pages about Doris Day, her movies and her recordings. No…she was not the only artist featured, but she was the one we used most. The students really liked her, too! It also afforded us the opportunity to visit New York City for a few days each year to attend the Columbia Scholastic Press Conference at Columbia University, where our humble newspaper received a 1st Place Award each year we attended.

Yes, I was a brave soul sponsoring 30+ students in their early teens for an overnight in New York. And I kept doing it for years. In fact, one year I took 34 students to Europe for three weeks, and it was one of the best experiences of my life. They remember it, too! In today's world, I would not be that brave.

Each spring at school, we also had a One Act Play Contest. Each grade produced a play to perform for the audience. The 9th graders produced two: one to perform as part of the contest, the other as an interlude while the judges picked the winners. Many of those years, I helped to direct several of the plays, especially when other teachers were not willing to participate. And the upper classes were not always the winners. In fact, one year I directed the 7th Grade Play and it won Best Play and Best Male Performer. (The kids and I were both euphoric about that!) Later, the Awards Presentation part of the evening was modeled after the Academy Awards. The only award not given was Best Director! Other than that, we followed the format pretty much, including stage design and costuming. The kids loved it. I was often found saying, "Do it like Doris Day". Back then, they knew what I meant. Years later, someone did not. That story…later!

Regarding Doris and awards, it is only fair to point out that it was only in one area that she seemed to not be favored…the Academy

Awards. They honored her with nominations (once for acting) and awards (at least three times) for her songs from movies. But other organizations presented her with honors every year from the 1950's through the 1960's. As far back as 1948, various groups honored her as Best Newcomer and by 1951, Photoplay pronounced her "Most Popular Female Star". Use your online access to see the various awards presented at *http://www.dorisday.net/box-office.html*. Another good source for this information would *be http://wwwimdb.com* (put in the movie title and check the awards listing). And by now, you are aware of the fact that no female movie star can match Doris' record as #1 Top Money Making Box Office Star of All Time. (Knowing that fact, one would think the Oscar gang would jump to give her An Honorary Award and an apology for overlooking her all those years when she reigned as Queen of the Box Office , but such is sadly not the case. Fortunately, groups like the Golden Globes, The Laurel Awards and Photoplay did not miss their opportunities. And Hollywood Columnist Liz Smith champions the cause every year!)

CHAPTER TWENTY-ONE:

REUNION TIME

It took two years for the folks in charge to reunite the most popular comedy team of all time. Doris, Rock and Tony were back in another frothy comedy that cleaned up at the box office. This time, it was called *Lover, Come Back*, and it grossed 17 million dollars and was one of the top box office films of the year. Motion picture exhibitors were well aware of the fact that any film starring Doris at this point in her career would clean up. The scripts should have been pouring out for them to do as many repeats as a team as possible while they were such a hot commodity (good business sense). But such was not the case. Fans and critics alike argue about which one was the better of the two films. *Pillow Talk* was inventive for introducing the split-screen imagery which became very popular, but *Lover* had a unique story idea about VIP (a nickel candy that was equivalent to several martinis).

Personally....I liked them both, and yet it took Hollywood three years to put this team together again! Talk about dragging your feet.

On the music front, Columbia released two albums by Doris. The first was a kind of sequel to *Cuttin' Capers*, and it was called *Bright and Shiny*. If you are ever feeling down or depressed, this is the one you want to play. It can lift your spirits just by playing the title song. But that is not all...Doris follows with some remarkable performances, all in a light and happy groove. Some of the great songs include: "I Want To Be Happy", "Keep Smiling, Keep Laughing, Be Happy", "Singing in the Rain", and a wonderful rendition of that peppy song from *South Pacific*, "Happy Talk." And that is just side one. The flip side begins with a song that I think explains Doris Day's philosophy of life, "Make Someone Happy". Other songs included are: "Riding High", "Sunny Side of the Street", "Clap Yo' Hands", "Stay With the Happy People" and "Twinkle and Shine".

This is a must have album for any collection with some sterling performances by Doris Day. I played this one almost every single morning in my classroom at school before the morning bell rang. It got me pumped up for the day, especially if I was not feeling as chipper as a teacher needs to be. (I had a little office in my classroom, complete with a record player and wall speakers.) And some of my early bird students used to come in, and we sat around and talked while we listened to the music and prepared for the day. In all my years of teaching, I found that students really liked to get to know the teachers they cared about. It was always pleasant to have a professional camaraderie with them. I liked getting to know them, and they liked that, too. We spent many hours together before and after school, when there was time, just chatting. It was so nice that there was time to do that.

Today, many of us are still friends and we converse on a fairly routine basis. For the most part, they still call me "Mr. DeVita"; or a shortened version, "Mr. D". The line of respect was never crossed in either direction. Facebook has helped to keep the lines of communication going. Some of my former students I haven't seen in years, but they have come to life on Facebook, and we are now back in touch. I am glad of that; I have missed them.

Besides the sunny personality and the often bright, chipper performances from Doris in movies and on records, she is most noted musically for the way in which she sings a ballad. How she can take any song and turn it into an experience in listening is always amazing. And there is no question about the fact that she is singing her song directly to the listener. Once Doris gets hold of a song, she makes it her own, and few can match that unique rendering. Listen to her version of Streisand's, "The Way We Were" as a perfect example.

Of course, I love all of Doris' music, and I have explained before that I cannot really select favorites. But I do have a couple of her albums that I have had to replace several times because I wore them out from playing them too much. I guess that should indicate their importance on my list. Such is the case with another great Doris album released by Columbia in 1961. It was called *I Have Dreamed*, and almost all of the songs have something to do with dreaming. The title song is one of the most beautiful versions of this tune from *The King and I* ever recorded, and even its writers (the team of Rodgers and Hammerstein) had nothing but praise for this interpretation by Doris. (Here is another show in which Doris could have starred in the film version. Deborah Kerr was good in the lead, but her singing was dubbed.) All of the songs in the album have the word "dream" in the title except four. "We'll Love Again" which was included because Doris really liked the song. She had sung it before (in 1956), but this was a new and lusher rendering. The other exceptions are "Time To Say Goodnight", "My Ship" and "Periwinkle Blue". The dream songs include: "I Believe In Dreams", "I'll Buy That Dream", "All I Do is Dream of You", "When I Grow Too Old To Dream", "You Stepped Out of a Dream", and "Oh What A Beautiful Dream." Lush is probably the keyword to explain the entire listening experience…lush and dreamy. A must have for your collection. And that title song is right up there with anything beautiful by Doris…yes, right up there with "Secret Love", an Oscar winner.

1961 was also a significant year for me because I started working my Master's Degree. By 1970, I would have more than one. I got one in Education/Guidance from University of Maryland. I got another in English from Johns Hopkins and then went back for their MLA (Master in Liberal Arts), where I had some outstanding world scholars as teachers, especially Phoebe

Stanton, known worldwide as an authority on all things associated with Art in architecture. She was a fan of anything gothic. This was a fun course with field trips and slides and interesting lectures. Dr. Stanton was a real trip: we dubbed her "The Barefoot Professor" because the first thing she did upon arrival to class was to kick off her shoes. We loved her, and I learned a lot about architecture as related to Art and culture. The Hopkins MLA program was among the first to be instituted as academic programs based on the history of ideas. It is a wonderful learning experience and is still in existence. Eventually, I ended up with enough degrees to be called "Dr. DeVita", but I did not relish or ever use that stuffy title.

Happy with my teaching career and looking for courses (required to keep teaching certificates current), the MLA Program was perfect for me. It exposed me to things with which I had little knowledge, including courses in sociology and psychology. (I steered clear of anything smacking of mathematics, always one of my weakest areas except for my first experience with Algebra 1, in which I got an "A"…the teacher was exceptional.) And yes, I still remember her name: Lois B. Stevens. You know how some teachers are engraved on your mind for various reasons. Funny, we never remember the mediocre ones, but we always remember the best, the worst and for some reason, the strictest. Miss Stevens was right up there with my all-time best list. These are the ones to whom I give credit for most of my career successes: Frances Shores Meginnis, Betty Beck, Emily Reimensnyder, Alfred Marsilio, Marion S. Sergeant, June Thearle and Phoebe Stanton. I will not honor the worst by listing them, but I had many.

Unfortunately, my list of inspirational *bosses* is very short. I had many bosses but few were inspiring. Maynard B. Henry tops my list. As a student, he was my principal in junior high school. As a teacher, he was my first boss. And he was delightful, inspiring and very supportive. One cannot ask for more than that in a boss.

CHAPTER TWENTY-TWO:

THE QUEEN AND KING OF COMEDY JOIN FORCES; MIKE'S NEW ADVENTURES

1962 was a different kind of year for Doris. She was in two very different films. A historical study of comedy in film will list all kinds of people, Doris included. On television, she may have taken a bit of a backseat to Lucille Ball, Mary Tyler Moore and Carol Burnett (although her five-year series was always in the Top Ten). In the movies, no one topped Doris' reign as Queen of the Comedy Film, especially romantic comedy. Sometimes, people forget that Doris got her training in comedy by starring with Bob Hope on his radio show. While she had natural comic timing, her tenure with one of the Kings of Comedy certainly did not hurt her. There were many kings of comedy. And in this year, Doris got to star with two of them.

First up was Cary Grant. Cary had starred in many romantic comedies in his career (as well as in some exceptional thrillers, thanks to Alfred Hitchcock). But as a King of Comedy, he had few competitors. Think: *Bringing Up Baby, Arsenic and Old Lace, His Girl Friday, The Philadelphia Story, Monkey Business, Mr. Blandings Builds His Dream House, I Was a Male War Bride, Houseboat, Operation Petticoat* and *Father Goose*, among others. He was a natural choice in 1962 to team with Doris, who was the current Queen of Comedy.

And it worked. *That Touch of Mink* was a box office smash and one of the top grossing films of the year, to the tune of about 15 million dollars. And from this movie come a few comedy routines that I always laugh about when I think of them. If you have seen the film, you will know what I mean when I mention them:

  - the hand slap through the slot in the automat

- Doris wiggling her toe on a champagne bottle
- the rash both of them developed at different times
- the computer room with paper flying
- Doris yelling in the baseball dugout with some baseball all-stars
- the elevator bed/the horse and carriage bed/the swimming pool bed, the bed that went everywhere

And many others. If you did not see this film, you should. It is the one which took Doris from the liberated woman of *Pillow* and *Lover*, and turned her image firmly into the constant Virgin. Many say this is the movie that got her that reputation that she could not shake even though the majority of her films after that portrayed her as a married woman, sometimes with children. What I remember mostly about this film was its rich color textures and the designer clothes, both male and female. What I missed? No music. Usually, a film with Doris could be counted on for at least one hit song. Nothing from this one. Nada.

But the next one made up for it. The comedy king this time was Jimmy Durante. Jimmy had starred on Broadway in the show known then as *Jumbo*. At the movies, it was called

Billy Rose's Jumbo. Other stars in the movie included Martha Raye and Steven Boyd. Some say this was a box office bomb. Interesting. It grossed almost 6 million dollars. While it was not as popular as *Mink*, it held its own. It was the last attempt by MGM at a big budgeted musical comedy (and the second time Doris appeared in an adaptation of a Broadway show.) Unfortunately for all concerned, the musical comedy was going out of favor by 1962. If this movie had been released two years earlier, it could have been a box office smash. As it was, it gave some great footage on what it is like to be part of a circus. And it had some wonderful songs. Steven Boyd surprised me with his rendition of "The Most Beautiful Girl in the World". I had no idea he could sing. And Doris provided us with two of her most beautiful recordings: "My Romance" and "Little Girl Blue", both of which were very stirring production numbers in the film. I loved *Jumbo* and have seen it many times. My students loved it, too. I had five classes that year, and I sponsored a trip to see the movie. Why? No special reason...I just thought the kids would enjoy it, and they did. (A couple of the girls cried through "Little Girl Blue"). Jimmy Durante and Jumbo, the Elephant, made a fun pair and provided quite a few of the film's jokes. Remember his line: "What elephant?" I am still laughing about that one. The soundtrack of the movie is one of my favorite albums by Doris, but two much more important albums were released by Columbia in 1962.

The first of these reminded people, once again, of Doris' foothold in the idiom of jazz. Anyone who has followed her career knows that Doris could do jazz singing with the best of them. After all, when she first started singing, she would sing along on the radio with Ella Fitzgerald and try to emulate her phrasing. She didn't need to bother… she had it all by herself. Listen to some of her early recordings with the Les Brown Band, specifically "Alexander the Swooze" and "Dig It". Then, listen to some of her earliest records when she first started her Columbia recording career. I refer to songs like: "Tulip or Turnip", "Pete" and "It Takes Time". I also think of "With You Anywhere You Are", "Put 'em In A Box, Tie 'em With a Ribbon", "Canadian Capers", "Say Something Nice About Me Baby", "No Moon At All" and "Now That I Need You". Doris could swing with the best. She always could, even when she first began her singing career with Barney Rapp at the "Sign of the Drum" or with Bob Crosby and his Bobcats on the road before her long term and often interrupted tenure with Les Brown and His Band.

And jazz it up she did with one of her most critically acclaimed albums, *Duet,* on which she performed with jazz pianist, Andre Previn and his trio. From such up-tempo numbers as "Control Yourself" and "Yes" to such standards as "Close Your Eyes" and "Wait Till You See Him", listeners can quickly see why she is listed today as one of the legendary singers of jazz. In fact, jazz artist Sarah Vaughan, when asked for her favorite singer, said, "I dig Doris Day".

I have to admit that at the time of its release, I was not a fan of jazz or jazz singing. I did not like Ella or Billie Holiday or even Mel Torme when they reverted to scat singing (something Doris never did, thank you). But I loved all of them when they sang an old standard and did it without improvisation. I also couldn't stand it when orchestras started playing progressive jazz, disguising the tune in such a way as to be completelhy and totally unrecognizable. Yes, I liked artists like Benny Goodman and Duke Ellington and the others when they played it straight and I knew what it was. The same goes for anyone else listed in the world of jazz. On this album, Doris got it right. I understood every track and liked them all. Andre and trio got to improvise a bit on the interim instrumental parts of the songs but never in a derogatory way. At its release, it was not one of Doris' most popular selling albums. I am not sure why because I know that it was played and played a lot on the radio, and especially on jazz-oriented stations. Deejays loved it. Today, it is one of her most consistent best sellers, especially on places like Amazon. And music critics still list it as one of her best records. As far as vocal jazz is concerned, it ranks among the very, very best. Any good critic will tell you that.

A little footnote here. *Until this album was released, I always liked Dinah Shore… certainly not as much as Doris, but I always enjoyed her TV show, and some of her hit records (like "Sweet Violets", "Chantez, Chantez" and "Shoo Fly Pie") were among my favorites. But on her TV show one evening, she slammed Doris big time. She had Andre Previn as a guest star and they were about to sing some of the same songs that Doris had recorded with Previn. They mentioned the "Duet" album, and Dinah said: "Let's sing those songs the way they should have been sung". That did it. I turned her off and I never turned her back on* *again. For me, Dinah Shore was now a dead issue. (Today, she actually is.) Also...although she might have made a guest appearance if asked (I doubt it), Dinah never asked Doris to appear as a guest on her show. I guess she was still jealous because Doris usurped her place as top female artist at Columbia Records back in the late 1940's. Eventually, Dinah moved to RCA Victor where she never became a really big artist again.*

Doris' other effort that year was in the realm of inspirational music. What a great amount of variety: Broadway, jazz and songs of faith. Wow...I keep saying, Doris can sing anything. She really can, and I have been saying that to my friends for years.

This third album was called "You'll Never Walk Alone", and it featured some very inspiring songs of faith...many old standards and many brand new songs written just for this venture. No one sings "Nearer My God To Thee", "Abide With Me", "Bless This House" or "In The Garden" like Doris. I fell in love with "I Need Thee Every Hour" and one of Doris' favorites, "If I Can Help Somebody". And the album close out, "The Lord's Prayer", is truly inspirational, as is the title song. This album was also a

215

favorite of my minister at church. In fact, at one Sunday service, he actually played it at the beginning and end of the formal Sunday services…I was in 7th Heaven (no pun intended.)

We certainly cannot say Doris stopped recording in the 1960's; she just no longer concentrated on single releases and did albums instead. She has said to me in correspondence of the time that singles by her kind of artist were no longer relevant; that rock and roll was at the mainstream, and that was not really her music. Me? I tend to disagree. I loved "Roly Poly" in *Pillow Talk*. I also liked some of her other attempts at rock and roll: "Whad'ja Put in That Kiss", "Two Hearts, Two Kisses" to name just two. There were others. We could also talk about a number of unreleased recordings that I personally think would have been hits. That comes in a bit. Just suffice it to say that I never thought Doris had a champion when it came to pushing her records. She needed someone like Terry to produce and sell her music! Face it: he did his thing for the Beach Boys, the Byrds, and others. He could have helped his Mom a lot! I think I suggested that in one of my letters to her back then. She never responded to that one. On second thought, maybe she did, she just never said it. That thought just came to me because in 1963, the very next year, one of her next best-selling albums (and one of my very favorites) was produced by her son. Hmmm...wonder if my suggestion had anything to do with that. One never knows!

As for me, 1962 was a significant year for a couple reasons. In the field of teaching, it is considered important to strive in an upward direction: department chairman, supervisor, administrator, principal and so on. I guess the powers to be don't realize that a regular classroom teacher who is successful in the classroom should stay right there and just continue to be an influential educator. I had no desire to leave the classroom.

My supervisors had other ideas. At that time, the innovators at our school were experimenting with a movement in education called "team teaching". The idea was to assign a specific number of students to a team of teachers who would then administer the program by moving the students back and forth to share each teacher's expertise. There were teams in English/Social Studies as well as in Math/Science, and there was one team on each grade level. In addition, some of the teachers crossed grade levels to teach certain subjects. (One example: I was considered an expert in the field of poetry. So…I taught students on all three levels various things related to that subject.) For a series of lessons, other teachers were brought in to cover such things as "Art During the Renaissance" (an Art Expert came in while her classes were covered by the assigned teacher) or "Renaissance Music" (an expert in music was brought in while his classes were covered). The idea was an excellent one (a forerunner of many kinds of things that were happening in various colleges). It was tried in several schools throughout the county with varying degrees of success.

The problem with the program concept is that all schools do not necessarily have teachers who can work in that situation and being assigned to it could cause disastrous results. That is why it was not successful in many schools. Where I was, we had visitors observing all the time because it was really successful. In my school, the principal (Maynard B. Henry) was exceptional. He knew his teachers very well, and he also knew who could and who could not work in that situation, as well as who could and who could not administer it. I was the English Team Leader, and I loved it. The supervisors took that in the wrong way and insisted that

I get a Master's Degree in Educational Administration and move up the ladder. I listened, and four years later, with degree in hand, I took on a Department Chairman job in another school with not so happy results…more on that later.

I said a couple things happened this year for me. At the time, I was living with my sister Roseanne in a not-so-great townhouse in a not-so-happy situation. She had left her cavorting husband and had no place to go with three children. She temporarily moved in with Mom and Dad. She was working full time, and my Mom and Dad could not really handle that large a brood in their home. So, they found her a place to live, hired a live-in baby sitter, and convinced me to move in with her and give her the rent I had previously given to them to help support the move. I agreed.

It really was not a good situation, and I was looking for a way out. I was friends with a girl named Carol, who was also teaching in the same school with me. She was in an impossible situation as well and was looking for a way out. So…getting married and moving in together was a way out, and we both opted for it. At the time, I did not know that I was not really interested in all the

219

things that go along with marriage. We stayed together four years, and then it was time to call it a day. I never ventured down that path again. I don't regret it. My heartfelt letters to Doris that year explained it all. She understood perfectly, and her responses were some things I truly treasured at that phase of my life. Doris has that effect on many people. She just understands.

CHAPTER TWENTY-THREE:

ROCK AND CARY STEP DOWN; ENTER JIMMY GARNER

In 1963, one of my all-time favorite Doris Day albums was released. It was produced and developed by Terry, and it reached the album *Hit Parade*...not very far up, but it still made the list. That usually means it is being played and heard and bought. It was certainly bought by me (ten copies...one for me, nine for friends: I believed in sharing when it came to Doris). And I guess I was thinking that if I bought a few copies, it might help to make the album a best seller! Yeah, right. My ten albums were not even a drop in the bucket, but I will say those who received them loved them and still have them....and still play them! As do I.

The album was called *Love Him.* It was an attempt on Terry's part to get his mother to sing some songs of the day, to get in the groove, so to speak, and show the world she could sing it all. And sing it she did. She sang Elvis: "A Fool Such As I", "Can't Help Falling in Love"; She sang Willie Nelson: "Night Life"; she sang Lenny Welch: "Since I Fell For You"; She sang Brenda Lee's hit, "Losing You"; She sang movie theme songs: "More" (theme from *Mondo Cane*); she sang current Broadway show songs: "As Long As He Needs Me" from *Oliver*; she sang Jack Jones: "Lollipops and Roses"…she sang everything, and the title song should have been released as a single: it could have hit the charts.

Coulda, woulda, shoulda….seems to be the theme regarding Doris songs in 1963. If you have not heard this album, you must. It is magnificent. Her versions of other people's hit songs are better than the originals. The addition of Tommy Oliver and his orchestra and chorus only punctuate the fabulous job Doris does on every one of these songs. I wrote to Doris four or five times that year praising this album; she always thanked me graciously. She is such a natural and so real.

Sometime in 1963, Doris went into the studios and recorded two songs that were never released in any form. Both could have hit the charts, one could have topped the charts. That one was called "Let The Little Girl Limbo" and the other was called "Oo-Wee Baby". Both were very commercial; both were never released. Again I say: coulda, woulda, shoulda. Where were you, Terry? "Limbo" was simply amazing, a lot like Eydie Gorme's one hit wonder, "Blame it on the Bossa Nova"…only much better.

Also in 1963, Doris connected with Robert Goulet for another album. At the time, Columbia was making studio releases of various Broadway shows featuring some of their top artists. For Doris and Robert, they chose *Annie Get Your Gun*. It was a great choice, and the music never sounded better. The studio album is done just like a regular soundtrack featuring an overture and finale and all the major songs from the show. Highlights include: "Doing What Comes Naturally", "You Can't Get a Man With a Gun" and a great duet on "Anything You Can Do, I Can Do Better". I like this version of the show better, in fact, than the original Broadway cast (Ethel Merman) and much better than the movie soundtrack (Betty Hutton). Years later, when I directed the show at Loch Raven Senior High School in 1982, we used the album by Doris and Robert to let the kids hear how the songs and accents should sound. Doris made a superb Annie (but then she had the former experience with this kind of singing part in *Calamity Jane*!).

The movies for Doris this year were two, and both were with then cowboy, James Garner, that handsome man from the TV cowboy show *Maverick*. When we talk about romantic comedy teams in Hollywood history, most teams are two people and that is it. In the case of Doris Day, she had two of them…first Rock Hudson and then James Garner, and both were very popular.

The first film was *The Thrill of It All*, a parody of TV commercials, and it topped the box office, grossing 12 million dollars. Doris' commercials for Happy Soap in this film are priceless, and some of the comedy effects are still memorable: a city of soap bubbles, driving the car into a pool that was not there in the morning, and Doctor Garner riding a horse to deliver a baby in a stalled car on the highway. Arlene Francis was fun in her supporting role as the rather mature expectant mother.

Then came Move Over, Darling. Originally supposed to be a film starring Marilyn Monroe and Dean Martin and called *Something's Got To Give*, it was re-tooled for Doris to co-star with James Garner, capitalizing on their popular pairing in the previous film. It, too, was a big success, grossing over 12 and a half million dollars in 1963. In one scene, Garner picked up Doris so quickly that he actually cracked a few ribs. Trooper that she was, she got it taped and was back to work the next day. They did not tell Garner until much later. He always remembers that to this day. And to this day, whenever the name of Doris comes up, Jimmy sports a broad smile and says, "I love Doris Day."

The title song was Doris' last single record to hit the pop charts, doing much better in the UK than it did in the US. The BBC in London banned it for being too suggestive. Doris Day…banned for being suggestive! Unbelievable!!! It didn't matter, though, because it was a big hit in the UK anyway, with or without the BBC.

When comparing the two teams (Doris and Rock/Doris and James), it is hard to select a favorite because they are different. I think both pairings are extremely convincing. Doris and Rock look great together, and in the movies as well as all the photos taken, they look like they really enjoyed each other's company. Doris always comments about how funny he was and how much he made her laugh. That is one thing Doris never talked much about with me in her letters…her co-stars. Today, that is very much a part of most of her current interviews. As for Doris and James, they look together like they are a long-term, happily married couple. Again, very convincing, and both teams were good choices. Although Hollywood history lists Doris and Rock as the most popular romantic comedy team, Doris and Jimmy were certainly a good pairing as well.

By now, most people know that Rock Hudson was a homosexual (or at least a bi-sexual if you believe Merv Griffin's book) and James Garner was a happily married man. They say that co-stars often fall in love while filming a movie. I believe that is something we will never know. Frankly, it is none of our business.

Side note:

I said that I would stop the story and let you know the minute I got a call from Doris. It

*happened on March 1, 2012 at 7:45 p.m.
We talked on the phone (she in Carmel, me
in Baltimore) for about 30 minutes, and we
talked about lots of things.*

*First off, she thanked me for the birthday
presents that I had sent well in advance so
she would have them in time. A box of
Berger cookies (her second one actually...I
had sent some before), a box of Wockenfuss
Chocolates (both of which are Baltimore
Institutions). She had eaten one or two of
them and said they were really delicious
(she loves candy and never gains any
weight). I also sent her a cute little
porcelain dog, and she said she loved it.
Last, but not least, was a home-made CD of
her singing the ten songs she recorded with
Buddy Clark...I thought she would really
like that (but she had not opened that part of
the package yet.)*

*We talked about Buddy, her first recording
co-star, with whom she had her first million
selling record, "Love Somebody". She said
he was a wonderful man, called him "very
sweet". Then she told me about his tragic
accident. He squeezed into a small plane
with five of his friends (because he was so
thin) to attend a football game. On the way
back home, after the game, the plane ran out*

227

of fuel, lost altitude and crashed on Beverly Boulevard. Buddy did not survive the crash. That was in October, 1949. Had he lived, I am sure they would have recorded many more songs together. No one else really became a recording co-star with her as successful as that team, although she did have some hit records later with Johnny Ray, Frankie Laine, Guy Mitchell, Donald O'Connor, Robert Goulet and others.

In the letter I had sent with the package, I told her about the death of my favorite cat, Mickey, at the age of 16, and my dilemma about replacing him. We still have his sister, Megan, who is also 16 years old, and has begun confusing our rugs for a litter box. I was unsure about bringing new kitties into that situation. Doris advised me to do it; she said that Megan would probably try to mother them and that might correct the other problem. I had not thought about that. Even if Megan does not last more than a few weeks or months, young new kittens would be resilient. On the other hand, if they saw Megan avoiding the litter box, they might think that is ok. I am not sure I am ready to find that out.

We also talked about her new puppy, which she named Squirrely Jackson. I reminded her that she had played a character named Dynamite Jackson in April in Paris. She laughed and said she had forgotten about that. I have always loved her laugh, and it sounded just like I remembered.

That led us to talking about the folks she misses most: her son, Terry; her mother, Alma; her brother, Paul. She said that they are still with her in spirit, and I firmly believe that. I told her that sometimes, in my mind's eye, I still see people and animals in my life that are long gone. She was not surprised at this comment and readily agreed that it is true. She said she wished that Terry could have been there to see how successful the new CD, My Heart, had become since he was instrumental in getting her to record those songs. I told her I am sure he is aware of it and smiling about it.

We talked about some of her movies, and she told me something I had heard before: that she never watches them. She did not want to see herself on the big screen because she would always think that she could have done something differently. She said she loved making movies while she did them. She also enjoyed the TV series (once she whipped the scenario into shape.) And the Best Friends show was not on long

enough. I told her about one of my favorites
of her songs, "I Didn't Slip-I Wasn't
Pushed-I Fell", and she did not remember it.
I promised her that I would send her a copy,
and I did. The fact that she did not actually
remember a song is not too surprising
considering she recorded almost 1000
songs.

I asked Doris if she would call into our
online website (www.sampod4u.com) on her
birthday this year since we are running a
special Happy Birthday Page. She said,
"Sure. Just send me the details I will need."
Trust me, I did send the details, and you will
be able to see if she called by checking the
website. If she does not, I understand. If she
*does, it is a wonderful bonus. (**Note: She*
did! The call is posted on the "Just Doris"
page.)

Doris sounded absolutely wonderful…that
same laugh I have loved for years, that same
voice I know so well. I told her I bet she
could still be a knockout on the big screen.
She laughed. I said she and Betty White
could do a great movie together, and she
laughed some more. Laughter…it is what
got Doris through all those tragedies in her
life, and there were many. It is what makes
her so important to so many people all over

the world. Her smile, her laughter, her positive outlook. A true angel, or as Frank Sinatra often called her, "a convention of angels".

And then we said our goodbyes, and she promised to call again. I cannot wait! I have waited to hear her "live" for over 66 years. It was well worth the wait.

CHAPTER TWENTY-FOUR:

ANOTHER ROMP WITH ROCK AND TONY; GUIDANCE AND BEYOND FOR MIKE

No one knows what took so long for the powers that be to reunite Doris with Rock Hudson and Tony Randall, considering their two previous films had been such box office blockbusters. Perhaps she had moved on, and it was more in to team her with Jimmy Garner as his wife.

Instead of independent career woman pursued, this time around she was already married to Hudson (who was a hilarious hypochondriac) and Randall was the next door neighbor. *Send Me No Flowers* (3 years later) was not a giant hit. Although it grossed 9.5 million dollars at the box office in 1964 dollars, it was a disappointment.

Doris was still Number One at the Box office, again. She, along with so many other big musical stars of the 1950's, was taking a backseat in the music singles department; this was, of course, the year of the British Invasion. Few major vocalists survived that musical attack. Me? I am sorry it ever happened. At the time, I never cared for The Beatles or The Stones or any of the other immigrants. Today, I can appreciate their contributions to the history of music. (I did like The Monkees, but they were a product of American television.)

The magic team of Day, Hudson and Randall had lost a little of the chemistry, and the story line of *Send Me No Flowers* was not as clever. That could explain why it is the one of the three films by this trio of performers that is not shown as often on TV when a Doris film is shown today. And no one knows why the team of Day and Garner was never again brought together: Doris and Jimmy had wonderful screen chemistry, and they are still very much in touch today. Although there were six more films to come in Doris' career, she would never again have a co-star to compare with Hudson or Garner…that was certainly Hollywood's loss.

I vividly remember the two albums produced by Doris in 1963. I can still picture the day I got *The Doris Day Christmas Album*. My wife and sister-in-law were going shopping. It was a Saturday (no school). All my work was caught up. I had the entire day to listen to and cherish this new album, and I did. I can't tell you how many times I played: "The Christmas Song" , "Have Yourself A Merry Little Christmas" and "I'll Be Home For Christmas". Years earlier, Doris had released a single version of another of my favorites from the album, but this version of "Silver Bells" was absolutely delightful. No one has ever sung it any better. Her versions of "Let It Snow" and "Winter Wonderland" are completely unique…unlike any sung by anyone else. I had never heard "Snowfall" before, but I loved it. "Toyland" was breathtakingly beautiful, and her version of Sinatra's "The Christmas Waltz" even became one of *his* favorites. "White Christmas" was also a new listening experience. There were two new songs written directly for the album that should have become Christmas classics: "Be A Child at Christmas Time" and "Christmas Present". She also gave us a really up-beat version of Les Brown's instrumental hit, "I've Got My Love To Keep Me Warm". Everyone I knew at the time owned this recording and loved it. It was not, for some unfathomable reason, one of Doris' Top sellers. It has been a consistent seller over the years in many different releases and compilations. The original album is no longer available. Some corporate bean counter needs his head examined!

For her birthday in 2012, Sony Music released a new, two CD album called *With A Smile and A Song* . But the first time Doris had an album called that was in 1963, which she recorded with Jimmy Joyce and His Children's Chorus. It was a truly infectious album, and Doris sounded wonderful with the kids. A couple of the songs from that album have been heard in various films during the past few years, especially "High Hopes" and "Zip-a-Dee-Doo-Dah". Some of the other great songs included are: "Give A Little Whistle", "Getting To Know You", "Nick Nack Paddy Wack", "The Lilac Tree" and "Do-Re-Mi", "Swinging On A Star", "Sleepy Baby", and the title song. In addition, there is a delightful new version of Doris' gigantic hit from 1956, "Que Sera, Sera". This album is still available; grab it while you can.

For me, this was also an interesting year. Because several of my teaching associates had done so, I thought that I might like to go into Guidance and have even a bigger effect on the students. I contacted the Guidance Office, and they approved my request. They had me start taking a series of special focused courses in conjunction with the Master's Degree on which I was working. They told me that, under no circumstances, would I be offered a job in Guidance until the degree was completed. Exactly two months later, I got a call offering me a job in Guidance at one of the schools in Baltimore County. It would start immediately because the person I would replace was leaving. I was totally shocked and not very happy. They were doing exactly what they said they would not do. And I turned them down. They told me if I didn't take it then, it would probably never be offered again. I still said no. *I hate liars!* So…I continued on with my degree in Educational Administration and Supervision from University of Maryland, which I received in 1966, with Guidance as a minor.

When I told Doris about this, she applauded my integrity. She always knew exactly what to say…it's no wonder I love her. In retrospect, I have discovered that Guidance Counselors do not have anywhere near the influence on students as do regular teachers.

No one has more positive impact on a student than a classroom teacher, except for a parent…and many parents don't have any positive impact at all. I know for a fact that some classroom teachers and their students end up becoming lifelong associates, many years after the teacher/student relationship has ended.

My Teaching Supervisor and Principal were both glad that I did not pursue the Guidance position…they wanted me to complete my degree and strive for a position as an English Department Chairman on the way to later becoming a principal or supervisor. That was to be my short-range goal. So…I continued teaching, planning, grading papers, advising the school newspaper and attending night school two nights a week and summers for the next few years. I had still worked as a counselor at Camp Wawayanda in the summer times until I started this degree. But this summer was to be the last year. The degree required two full-time summers on the college campus. That did not make me happy; I missed the camp experience. And I never went back to it. I miss it still. After a few years, you really can't go back. Somehow, it is never the same. I guess that is true with anything in life. The adage is: "you can't go back", and it is so true. Now…if we had time travel for real…..no, it still wouldn't be the same, methinks. That "can't go back" idea certainly showed itself throughout Doris' movie career and after. When she stopped, she stopped. As her son always said, "She knew when to move on. She did it very well."

CHAPTER TWENTY-FIVE:

SOME THINGS OLD; SOME THINGS NEW

When reviewers and historians talk about Doris' film career and her successful co-stars, they rarely mention Rod Taylor. Frankly, I am not sure I understand why not. They also say her popularity began to decline in those years. Nothing is further from the actual truth. Facts are facts.

In 1965, the film was *Do Not Disturb* and in 1966, it was *The Glass Bottom Boat*. They both paired Doris with Rod. They both scored respectively at 8 million and 9.8 million dollars, not cheap change in the profit market of those years. In 1964, Doris was still #1 at the box office, and in 1965, she was #3 following Sean Connery and John Wayne, but still the #1 female, just *ahead* of Julie Andrews, who won Best Actress that year for *Mary Poppins*.

Personally, I loved the chemistry between Doris and Rod Taylor. They looked natural together, in the first film as husband and wife, in the second as mermaid and pursuer. One of the funniest scenes in any of Doris' comedy films takes place in *Disturb* when she is slightly inebriated and does a one woman routine to "Au Revoir is Goodbye With A Smile"…that scene alone is worth the price of admission. Doris' energetic performance and some of the most beautiful outfits she has ever worn in any film since *Pillow Talk*, including a drop-dead gold evening gown, clearly indicating that she was one of the silver screen's sexiest actresses…..something not often mentioned. It may have taken Ross Hunter with *Pillow Talk* to show off the Doris Day physique, but it was not overlooked in this movie or the next one when she was wearing her mermaid costume. *The Glass Bottom Boat* continues to be a favorite movie of Doris fans, as well as with viewers of Turner Classic Movies, who run it often, usually by request. The film also brought back a previous TV superstar, Arthur Godfrey, who plays Doris' father. They do a fatiguing rendition of the film title song, and a brief duet on "Que Sera, Sera" (a third time for the song in a Doris film—first in *The Man*

Who Knew Too Much; second in *Please Don't Eat The Daisies*.)

On the music front, 1965 was the year when Columbia released two of my favorite Doris albums...I had no idea that they would be her last two studio albums. They were a perfect combination of old and new.

New was a Doris entry into the world of bossa nova. It was called *Latin for Lovers*, and no one...literally, no one...can sing it better. The amazing orchestration was produced by Mort Garson, but the voice was vintage Doris in a new direction. It begins with "Quiet Nights of Quiet Stars" followed by a truly inspired interpretation of "Fly Me To The Moon". Put this record on when you want to entrance someone else, turn off the lights, light a candle or warm up the fire place, and watch out. Doris then moves deftly through "Meditation", "Dansero", "Summer Has Gone", "How Insensitive" and "Slightly Out of Tune". Then it is time to take a popular Hit Parade song and put it in a bossa nova beat: "Our Day Will Come". Two traditional Latin favorites included are: "Be True To Me" and "Be Mine Tonight". There were two songs in the album that should have been released as singles. They could have been big hits. I humbly refer to

241

"Perhaps, Perhaps, Perhaps" and "Por Favor". "Perhaps" has even been used in some contemporary films as well as for a remix in some disco clubs. In a recent television interview, Betty White talked about Doris' sexuality as a singer and how it often got her into trouble. She was talking about Doris' first big single hit, "It's Magic". I would love to hear her talk about this album!

Then comes something old and new combined. The album was fittingly called *Doris Day's Sentimental Journey* and Mort Garson was once again the arranger and conductor. This time it was a nostalgic trip for Doris back to the 1940's, when her musical career began. It was a chance for her to sing some of the songs she had sung with the Les Brown Band ("Come To Baby Do", "It Could Happen To You", and of course, the title song), only this time the focus is on the singer and not the band--- wonderful new arrangements with lush orchestrations. Doris had told me in one of her letters that she loved having the chance to sing some of the songs again, especially ones that she felt deserved better treatment. She also had the opportunity to record some of her favorite songs from that era that she had sung before but never recorded. Songs like: "The More I See You", "At Last", "I Had The Craziest Dream", "It's Been A Long, Long Time", "I Don't Want To Walk Without You", "I'll Never Smile Again" and "I'm Beginning To See The Light" form the major focus of the album. She also does a truly wonderful nod to the music of Glenn Miller with "Serenade in Blue". There are renditions of songs in this album that have never been sung any better by any musical artist. When Doris did her *Day By Day* album in the 1950's, considered one of her very best, she sang my all-time favorite song of hers, "I Remember You". It was wonderful then; the new rendition of the song in this album is simply breathtaking. To top it off, she re-does that first really monster hit from the days with Les Brown, and it truly is a sentimental journey for all her listeners. This is an album to play again and again and again and again. It was her last known studio album recording with Columbia, and it was magnificent.

In my world, things were topsy-turvy. My marriage was anything but, and it was time for us to call it off, which we did at the end of 1966. In fact, I actually spent January 1, 1967 moving into a new apartment in Cockeysville, Maryland. It was a clean and amicable break and came at a convenient time. I had just finished one of my graduate degrees and was offered the job as English Department Chairman in a newly-opened school. So, I not only started a new career, but a new beginning as a single man at 30 years of age. When I told Doris about this, her retort was wonderful. She congratulated me on the promotion and added, "I know all about divorce."

Sometime in 1967, Doris went in to Columbia Studios to record an album of some of her all-time favorite tunes. The brass did not approve of the selection, but Doris won out. Unfortunately, that was when her husband, Marty, became very ill. The tapes for the album were put aside while Doris spent an awful lot of her free time caring for her estranged husband (they were not as close then as they once had been). Movie-wise, that was the year that Doris did her first real cowboy/western film (not counting *Calamity Jane*, which was a musical). It was called *The Ballad of Josie* and co-starred Peter Graves, George Kennedy, and that perennial cowboy star, Andy Devine. Doris played a young woman who stirs things up in a western town by raising sheep instead of cattle and organizes the local women to demonstrate for women's suffrage. No, she still was not playing a movie virgin, despite the image and all that was written about her. The movie didn't tear up the box office, but by then, Doris fans would see her in anything and the picture grossed 8 million dollars. It was probably my least favorite of her movies, but still a fun one to watch. The chemistry with Peter Graves was also a plus.

That was also the year that Doris starred in *Caprice*, a comedy spoof on the then extremely popular James Bond films. It certainly was a timely film; it had a cast of very popular costars featuring: Richard Harris, Ray Walston, Edward Mulhare and Michael J. Pollard. However, it only grossed 4 million dollars instead of the usual 8 or more.   I remember not liking it very much, and Doris didn't either. It was one of those films, like *Josie*, that her agent had signed her to do without her approval. It was the first time that Doris dropped out of the Top Ten list of money-making stars, but she still retains that title as Top Money-Making Female Star in the history of the movies. Everyone can have a not so great film, even though both films made a respectable amount of money. One thing remained constant: Doris never gave a bad or shoddy performance -- she gave it 100 percent always, regardless of how she personally felt. This is true of her films as well as her music and all the other endeavors in her life.

My first year as a Department Chairman in a brand new school was interesting, to say the least. The building was shaped much like the letter "E" with one additional side. In other words, there was only one main hall which included the offices, nurse and guidance department. Then there were four side halls which we designated as A, B, C and D. Because the major high school for the area had just opened and it was already very overcrowded, they needed some place to house their 10th Graders until they could accommodate them. So, Hall D of our school was set off as The Tenth Grade Hall. Meanwhile, the local elementary school was also having growing problems and they needed a place for two first grades and a third grade. So, Hall A became The Elementary Wing, the 7th Grade Wing, and the main area for specialists such as the Remedial Reading and Special Education Teachers. That left B and C for the 8th and the 9th Graders. We called the school Cockeysville Junior Senior High School (with a little elementary thrown in)! As head of the English Department, I was responsible for all of these when it came to this subject.

I had a wonderful and very supportive principal the first year. I only had four classes, instead of the usual five (because I had two periods a day for department business: supervising/assisting teachers, handling administrative details, attending meetings, etc.) Those who know anything about teaching know that it is rare for a department head to have his or her own classroom; instead they traveled (or "floated") to various rooms throughout the building to teach their classes in someone else's room. The students at my previous school knew this would happen, so as a farewell gift, they gave me a podium on wheels which had a plug in light on top and three shelves inside for carrying things. This was a Godsend! I actually taught in several classrooms in all four halls during the course of each day, and packing my traveling podium became a daily occurrence. The students used to tease me about how fast I traveled to get from class to class in under 5 minutes. They also supplied a horn to ward off slow walkers in front of me as I speeded down the halls.

This was also the year in which I finally was able to give up the school newspaper (whew!); unless you really love it, producing a newspaper is not a fun or an easy job. I was able to convince one of my teachers to take on the job, and I helped just the first year. After that, she was on her own. She did not complain much because it gave her an extra period free for the paper, a little additional salary, and one less class to teach as compensation.

This was also the year that sparked my interest in theatre arts. Previously, I had directed one act plays once a year, and that is how this interest began. We had a unit on plays in the English Curriculum, and one of the things we studied was the early roots of theatre, the Greek Play, and we acted out (instead of just reading) *Antigone* in class. The class enjoyed it so much they talked me into producing it as an actual play in the school "cafetorium" (just like it sounds, a cafeteria with a stage and curtain and lights, etc.). One member of the class knew about lighting so he handled that. Togas were simple enough costumes (everyone had sheets at home). One of the students was able to do make-up. So… we did one performance on a Friday night, and believe it or not, people actually came to see it. (It may have helped that we did not charge admission!) A Greek one act play became my first experience in true live theatre.

The next year we produced another of the plays we did in English class, the longest running non-musical in the history of Broadway theatre, Clarence Day's *Life With Father*, which was written and dramatized by Howard Lindsay and Russell Crouse from a series of essays by Clarence Day, Jr. taken from real life.

This time, we actually had open auditions, cast it and did actual rehearsals. This was also the beginning for me of those night rehearsals. We would rehearse one or two nights a week and occasionally on a Saturday or Sunday afternoon (to avoid conflicting with the various sports schedules which took place almost every day after school). This arrangement meant that students were not forced to choose between athletics and theatre…this way, they could do both. It did not hurt that major school jocks were also performing on the stage! It was a policy I followed for the next 20+ years. It only caused me a problem many years later in high school. We were having dress rehearsal for the play we were doing at the time, and a cancelled meet for the cross country team was rescheduled for the same night as our dress rehearsal. My policy was: miss a dress rehearsal and someone else plays your part. It involved two male students. I am happy to say they chose the play over the meet, and I gained the respect of that coach for the rest of my tenure in teaching.

But for *Life With Father*, we actually did Victorian costuming, pasty-looking makeup, and a real set design. In fact, when the audience arrived and the curtain opened, there was an audible "wow" as they reacted to the beautiful Victorian set in rich red and gold colors, complete with truly authentic furniture, thanks to our then Art Chairman and Set Designer, Starr Coale. One of the jokes in the beginning of the play is the entrance of each member of the Day family. As each enters, the hair color gets redder and redder. We only had one member of the cast who actually had red hair. You know what we did; everyone died their hair several times to get the proper look. And we double cast (all the parts were played by two people, one for Friday Night and one for Saturday Night, thus ensuring good attendance for both nights.) The house was packed both nights (many were repeaters who wanted to see the opposite cast); we were a success, and I started down the new road to directing plays for the next 24 years of my career. That job was always a team effort. I was always lucky enough to have wonderful helpers and assistants every year, and sometimes these helpers were former students, which I loved as you can probably guess. There were also some parents along the way who helped in the effort.

I was also fortunate enough at that school to convince my principal to offer "Speech and Theatre Arts" as an elective subject for the tenth graders while they were still housed at the school. (Both Speech and Theatre Arts were offered in most high schools as 3-period per week electives; by combining both, we were able to meet five days a week.) And I really enjoyed teaching those classes.

CHAPTER TWENTY-SIX:

TROUBLE, TROUBLE, TROUBLE AND A WAY OUT

Frankly, I will never understand how Doris did as much as she did in 1968 without completely falling apart. In that year, she completed what would be her last two movies; helped her husband as he battled illness and watched helpless as he passed away; began the long legal journey of what ended being a 99 day trial; all the while she was preparing for her first foray into the world of television. (I guess it should not come as a surprise to any true Doris fans. 39 films in 20 years is a record for anyone and five of them in one year! Doris really could handle just about anything.)

Where Were You When the Lights Went Out was another of those films Doris was forced to make because of her agent had approved the script, which was not great. About this film, Doris has said, "This alleged 'comedy' was the worst film I ever made." The premise of the film was based on New York's 1965 power failure which threw the entire city and much of the East Coast into darkness. The shock and confusion of the blackout was well depicted by re-creations of New York landmarks, traffic jams, computers gone haywire and what erupted as a result. It might also be important to point out that during the filming, Doris spent much of her time in traction having pinched a nerve in her back. Also, the film is noted for a not so good "in joke", that being the character which Doris played was starring in a play called *The Constant Virgin* (here we go again). The movie still managed to gross 7.9 million dollars. Certainly much of the film's success can be attributed to Doris' usual attitude about giving 100 percent. It also helped that she had co-stars of high caliber like Patrick O'Neal, Robert Morse, Terry Thomas, and other comedic giants: Steve Allen, Jim Backus, Ben Blue and Pat Paulson.

Consider these things and again wonder at how Doris managed it all. That movie was released in March, Marty died in April, and her next film was released in August, not long after she discovered she had no money and was deeply in debt. She had also been signed up for a television show without her knowledge, and advances were paid for her appearances.

Previous encounters with television for Doris were primarily as guest appearances on such shows as *What's My Line* and *The Ed Sullivan USA Chat Show* in the 1950's and her annual appearance at the Oscars in 1958, 1959 and 1960. She had never wanted to do television but she did not go back on her word and the series began a successful five-year run which started in September of 1968. It was that series that helped her pay off her debts and get back on her feet.

But first, let's back up to August and the release of another of Doris' most popular films, her last, *With Six You Get Eggroll*. The film grossed over 10 million dollars in 1968. Had the obviously unwanted TV series not happened, this film could have been the start of a whole new movie career, with Doris now taking on the parts of mature women. Doris plays a widow with three sons who becomes involved with a widower with a daughter. The hostile reaction of the kids to their dating and marriage is the focus of the film which contains some of Doris' best comedy scenes in years. Brian Keith was her capable co-star, and the cast list included such stellar comedy performers as George Carlin, Jamie Farr, Alice Ghostley, William Christopher and Pat Carroll. It has often been compared to the Lucille Ball film, *Yours, Mine and Ours*, which is nowhere near as funny. No one knew it would end up being her last film, least of all Doris. But other things got in the way for a long time.

The Doris Day Show was one of the top 5 shows in the ratings for its first year when it opened the Fall Season in September of 1968. It stayed in the money for five years and ended when Doris decided not to sign again at the end of the season in 1973. Doris said, at the time, "I have done all that can be done with the material for this show, and I am not interested in working on it any longer." In effect, she was cancelling her show, even though CBS was ready to sign her to another year.

The show focused on Doris as a working widower named Doris Martin. It stressed Doris' role as a comedienne. In that respect, it was every bit as good as the Lucille Ball or the Mary Tyler Moore Shows. With the exception of the opening credits, during which Doris sings a few bars of "Que Sera", there was little if any focus on singing. After all, Doris played Doris Martin, a working woman, not a singer. (A couple notable exceptions: a guest appearance when Doris Martin interviews Tony Bennett and he has her sing along on a chorus of "I Left My Heart in San Francisco" and the annual Christmas Shows on which she sings various carols with her costars.)

The show was known most for its change of venue most seasons. Doris started as a widow on a farm with Pop and two kids, and ended up in a glamorous apartment in San Francisco sans father and kids. Not much was done to explain away the changes, but Doris was determined to work on it until it became a better show. Most fans agree that the third and fourth seasons were the best. The fashion shows presented on some of the episodes can be seen to this day, mostly on YouTube.com.

Personally, I cannot say I was as fond of the TV shows as I was of the movies. This was back in the days before I had any means of recording the shows. By this time, I was into night rehearsals for the school drama and musical productions. With that and the added burdens of teaching, I did not always get to see many of the shows. And I felt like

256

I was deserting my favorite person. I told Doris this in one letter I wrote; her response was what I expected. Today, I own the entire series, and I watch fairly often, especially the ones featured on sampod, my website.

What I personally liked a lot better were the specials produced by CBS (which was part of the deal worked out between them and Marty). The first of these Doris called *The Doris Mary Ann Kappelhoff Special* with guest stars Perry Como and Rock Hudson in 1971, while the weekly TV show was still running. The show was wonderful and a ratings success. Doris did what she does best in this show…sing! She sang a great duet with Perry Como of many standard tunes and each did one or two of their hits. She had a very unique opening medley and ended the show doing a stand up song routine of "Sentimental Journey" and "It's Magic", both with sparkling new, polished arrangements. In between, there was a fashion show featuring "Sexy Doris" as well as some great song and dance numbers. The show, with some cuts and additions, would have been a great one for Las Vegas, but Doris was not doing in person appearances. What a shame. This is where Doris should have headed…a weekly special like that

would have been absolutely terrific or a
show in Vegas. Broadway would have been
great, too.

It was mentioned that Steven Sondheim was
trying to get her for the lead in *Follies*.
Instead, he settled for a Doris-type in
Dorothy Collins from the old *Your Hit
Parade* days. This time around, I was able
to record the special. I still have the original.

Ever the busy bee, at about the same time, in
1971, Doris was beginning to do active work
as an animal activist. She had always loved
animals, especially dogs, and maintained
quite a few of them in her home. She felt it
was time to lend her name to some animal
causes and she got involved in Actors and
Others For Animals. That led to her own
establishment , The Doris Day Pet
Foundation (DDAF) in 1977. It is famous
around the world for its humanitarian work
with animals in need. Spay Day USA was
begun by Doris when she worked with the
Humane Society of the United States and is
now an annual event. This also led to the
establishment of the Doris Day Animal
League, a legislative arm of her organization
to lobby Congress in areas of animal health
and protection. That is the main focus of her

time today, and it occupies every waking moment. Now, back to 1974.

Her next special appearance on TV was on the John Denver Show where they did some great tunes together. They also did a number of spoofs on their respective images in some fun comedy routines. It was another ratings winner, as was her final special in 1975.

That one was called *Doris Day Today*. Her guest stars included: Rich Little, Tim Conway, and John Denver. One of the highlights from the show was a *Sunshine Medley* with John. Also, a comedy interlude in which Little plays various of Doris' co-stars from her films. Doris sings a beautiful version of "The Way We Were" with great background shots of her film co-stars all through the years fading in and out. Still another ratings success, and still another I was able to record.

Doris may not have been making movies any longer, but she certainly was not resting on her laurels, so to speak. (Considering the fact that she won so many Laurel Awards through the years, she could have!)

Instead, she had decided she wanted to write a book and tell her real story, not the one as

"The Girl Next Door" or "The Constant Virgin" for which she was acclaimed. She contacted noted author A.E. Hotchner. He was reluctant to do it because he was sure there was nothing to tell. When she told him she wanted to tell the whole story, no stones unturned, he agreed and *Doris Day-Her Own Story* became a #1 Best Selling book in 1975. Her in-person guest appearances on every major talk show (from Johnny Carson to Barbara Walters, as well as Vicki Lawrence and Phil Donahue) helped to keep the book alive.

Doris continued to work on her television series, taking an active part. She (and son Terry) continued to amass materials to help in the court trials to come with Jerry Rosenthal, the financial manager who never ever acknowledged his onerous guilt. There was talk of several rendezvous between Doris and various co-stars on the show, just like there has always been about Doris and any co-stars. If any of the talk is true, that's great. True or not...it is not any of our business. For my part, I hope she had a few really steamy love affairs with some very nice men...she deserved them after Marty.

After the success of the book and the end of TV shows, Doris kind of disappeared. Not completely, but in a different way. She surfaced from time to time at various events that benefitted animals in some way. But her performing days were over. She never said that she retired. She just moved on to something else that occupied her time completely. As her son said, "She always knew how to move on."

For me, 1967 through 1970 were a whirl. I can think of no other word for it. We produced my first directed musical, for which we chose the fun MGM musical turned play, *Good News*. It was almost a total school effort. The Music Department Chairman was our Musical Director and Orchestra Leader; several members of the English Department helped with costumes, makeup and directing; and the super Art Department did sets and scenery. The Mechanical Arts Department handled lights and curtain. And we did a program complete with patron ads that brought the school much needed dollars (shared by all the departments involved). Once more, we did double casting to ensure a nice, two-night turnout. We had a completely packed house both nights.

I am still in close touch with one of the stars from this show. He had played Clarence Jr.

in *Life With Father* and now was one of the leads in this show. His name is Dan Funk. I will talk about him again. He was just an amazing all around student and one of the most talented natural performers with whom I have ever worked. Today, he produces and directs various projects in Los Angeles, California. Unfortunately, he is no longer on the stage, where he could be. I have asked Dan in his current position of influence to try to get Doris back on TV, at least for a current interview. He says he is still working on that one. If anyone can do it, he can. But I won't hold my breath. Trust me, I know my friend Doris. And she means it when she says "No". (Ask Oprah Winfrey about that one!)

At some point during this three-year period, our school got a new principal, when our previous leader was promoted. The new King of the Block was a Queen. I have had many female bosses and supervisors in my life, and I enjoyed most of them. Such was not the case with this one. I will not even honor her by listing her name. She was a strong woman. Very strong! And she did not like strong men. And so, for the better part of three years we battled. But mostly, we battled about our divergent philosophies of educational administration (it was I who had the most recent degree in the subject, not she). With my teaching, she had no fault. She continued to give me superior evaluations. Such was not the case in my position as Department Chairman. (The members of my own department evaluated me favorably every year.) In her case, we disagreed on one very important point.

I believed that my job was to assist my teachers in any way I could. If they needed help, they got help. If they needed praise, they got that, too. She felt that it was my job to evaluate them in such a way that she could get rid of them if they did not do the kind of job she wanted. In fact, on several occasions, she told me to go visit and evaluate two particular teachers and write negative reports, which I refused to do. On several really good teachers, we totally and completely disagreed, and I would not help her to get rid of them by writing negative evaluations. In one case, she objected to the teacher's obesity and felt that we should encourage her to leave the classroom and go on a diet. (Can you imagine the gall???) When I told her I would not do that, she suggested I look for a school where the principal agreed with me. And I did. I should have reported her to someone, but I opted to just get rid of an intolerable situation. When I left, the majority of my department members were not happy, but they never knew the whole story. The Vice Principal thought I should fight her with the Board of Education, and he offered his support. I did not really want to make waves.

So I did a lot of soul searching. And then I realized something very important that many teachers overlook today. I asked myself why I went into teaching. The answer is to teach not to supervise. So I very quickly contacted my former principal (Maynard B. Henry, who was always a pure joy) from my first school, and he said if there was no position available that next year, he would make one. So I went back to my former school, Towsontown Junior High School, until it closed years later. In retrospect, one year later, I was told there was only a handful of men still on the faculty of the school which I had left, all of them "yes men". That very strong woman had a lot of well-behaved sheep.

Once again, in my correspondence with Doris, she was very supportive. In these last few years, our usual correspondence became spotty. Suffice it to say, we were both very busy. I never neglected complimenting her on her new projects or telling her about mine. One thing was certain: Doris always responded. It may not have been in a week or two, but a response was always in the offing. This is still true today. Along with the gigantic amount of time she spends today on animal activism, she has an equal amount of time devoted to fan mail, which still comes in bags and boxes on a daily basis.

Returning to my previous school was just what the doctor ordered. The principal saw to it that I had the cream of the crop, the best students in the school. If another teacher complained about that, he sent them on a round of teacher observations. For some reason, they stopped complaining.

I had also agreed to set up a full-time theater operation, without having a class to teach in the schedule. We used the cafeteria and started doing two shows a year in the round. We were able to order risers on which to build up the stage and lights, and we were set. With the able assistance of the Art and Music Departments and great assists from students who knew how to build sets, we managed to knock out some very popular shows in the next few years. Some of these included: *Dracula*, *The Sound of Music*,

Meet Me in St. Louis, *The Bad Seed*, *Li'l Abner* and many others. We built up a very respectable drama program, along with a good reputation. I had always told the kids that if someone tells you "this was a really good show", be proud, because that was usually the truth. However, if they add, at the end, "for a junior high school", that was definitely not a compliment. I wanted them to perform like it would be in a Broadway production…and they mostly never let me down.

There was one show, though…..Agatha Christie's *Mousetrap*. That was not a good experience…and I punished myself 2 more times by trying it again in two different situations. It never worked. So I now believe that show belongs in London, where it has its record as the longest running non-musical.

I must add that I was very lucky. In every school where I produced theatrical productions, we made money….a lot of money. The majority of principals with whom I worked had the philosophy that if we made the money, we could spend it. Spend it we did on lights, makeup, sound, costumes, etc. By the time the school closed in 1978, we had a theatrical system the envy of many high schools and colleges in the area, and we took it all with us to our next school, which had next to nothing.

I formed a kind of partnership with the teacher in the room next door to me. Her name was Mary Lou Arthur. I had a classroom with a stage (how fitting) and a room which could easily hold 60 people. She had a regular classroom which held about 35. So, we started our own teaching team, moving the kids back and forth from room to room, sometimes in single groups, sometimes as a whole. Oftentimes, we did a lesson in tandem, she covering one aspect of a subject and me another. The kids loved it, and so did we. It made teaching a great deal of fun for everyone. This kind of thing started happening all around the school, and soon we were sharing lessons on various grade levels all over the building. It was a great time to be a teacher. But good things don't necessarily last forever. Mr. Henry retired in 1976 after fifty plus years in education, and in came the second worst principal I had ever seen.

 His replacement came from the local Board of Education's Guidance Department, he complete with a Doctor's Degree (most likely in Education…degrees that were a dime a dozen.) Later, I was told they had eliminated his position in Guidance in order to transfer him elsewhere (because once that happened, they reinstated the job with someone else a year later.) The man may have had a doctoral degree, but he had no common sense. He thought that he needed to fix something that wasn't broken. He came into one of the best schools in the entire County, and he managed, in two years, to create the biggest morale problem I have ever seen. The faculty even got up a petition to have him recalled. Of course, that didn't work, and he never let them forget it. The Board of Education wisely decided to close the school at the end of the school year in 1978, thus dispersing to all sections of Baltimore County one of the most closely knit teaching staffs in any school around.

For my next school, I chose what was known as Loch Raven Middle School: they had no drama program, no stage…but they had a very nice cafeteria! The principal wanted a drama program. Once again, Doris applauded my decision. (Yes, we were still corresponding, but it was now in short notes.) By the way, the old school was slightly remodeled and reopened later as Carver School of Technology and the Arts.

CHAPTER TWENTY-SEVEN:

DORIS DISAPPEARS AGAIN; MIKE HAS A NEW BEGINNING

After 39 films in 20 years, hundreds of recordings, 5 years on television, a best-selling biographical book, and two television specials, Doris seemed to disappear from the face of the earth, at least as far as the public eye was concerned. That really was not the case. She moved avidly into her new chosen line of work, that of animal advocacy. She wisely decided to use her name and star power to champion causes for those who cannot speak for themselves. Her neighbors were well aware of her cause. And if a person was not treating an animal properly, Doris did not hesitate to let them know. At that time, the expression was: "Treat your animals right or Doris Day will get you!" Her name may not have been in the papers and magazines as often now that she was no longer filming or recording, but she was definitely not in hiding.

She married for the last time in 1976 to Barry Comden, the maître d' at one of her favorite restaurants. Barry convinced Doris to sell her home in Beverly Hills and build a new home in Carmel, California (the seaside resort she had fallen in love with while filming *Julie*). If that had not happened, there is every possibility that Doris might have eventually made more films. The distance from Carmel to L.A. made it easy to not return. As for Doris, she did not talk much about Barry. She simply said she really did not know how to pick a husband. In our correspondence during those years, he was never mentioned. And yes, we were still corresponding. You might wonder why I never hopped a plane to go visit. Frankly, it never crossed my mind. Had I received an invitation, I might have considered it.

For me, 1979 and 1980 were busy times indeed. Starting in a new school is always a major operation, especially when building a new program. In this case, the only familiar thing for me was that I was still teaching 9th graders in a junior high school. Beginning a new theater program in a cafeteria without a stage meant back to risers and lights, and moving tables and bringing in chairs for two weekend shows. The physical table and chair movement had to take place for every rehearsal as well so that the student actors could perform on an actual stage. This was perhaps the most challenging of all stage venues because half of the cafeteria area was cut up; there was a faculty dining room in the middle of the cafeteria. (We used that for make-up and dressing rooms for the shows.)

Two things were significant about this school for me, one of which Doris enjoyed hearing about. That was the one class that I had which totaled 29 boys. I guess the vice principal knew me too well; he felt that I could do something with this group of 29 students who had been trouble makers ever since they started in that school as 7th graders. They took one look at their short teacher and thought they would have the upper hand. But I was tough, at least at first. They balked, but eventually they came around.

The true test came when we got to the drama units. As both an English and Theater teacher, I never let the students just read a play; we acted it out. I thought there might be a problem when I asked the guys to read the women's parts. It wasn't, and some of the most macho guys in the school actually enjoyed trying their skill in a female role. (That is, once they understood that in Shakespeare's time, all the actors were male.) Of course, the highlight was the week we did *Romeo and Juliet* and the balcony scene. When we got to that, the most popular boy in the entire school, known for his macho image, read the part of Juliet, using his jacket as a dress. It was a riot, and we all got a good laugh. (No one took any incriminating pictures, and the only guest to view the play was the vice principal, who also enjoyed it.) Once we got the silliness out and continued the play till the very end, no one even thought about the fact that it was male or female; it was a sad ending and acted properly. This teacher was very proud of this class of all boys; they came a long way that year. (I might add, there was one day that was a problem. That was the day that the principal added a female to the mix in the class. By the time the period ended, I knew this group would not have the same camaraderie if she remained. They would have to show off for a girl and revert to their "oh so macho" images. So I did my part to have her moved elsewhere and told the powers that be that the group needed to stay as is. It did.) The other plus was that some of these boys who had received very low grades in 7th and 8th grades, were now getting B's and A's. I was like a proud father, and they knew it. I still miss them today. Teaching that class for me had been a true joy and a real experience. I should add that it met every day during the last period of the day, the toughest time to learn a major subject.

The other of the two things was one of the two vice principals. The one I mentioned earlier was familiar and a friend (he had actually come to this school with me from the previous school). The other had been one of my math teachers when I was in high school. He was in charge of the cafeteria, and he did not like, not in any way, the fact that we were taking his domain and using it for plays in the evenings. He had a real problem when we started installing lights. It took two years, but by the time the end of the second year came around, he became a convert. Let's just say he learned the difference between two words: *plays* and *theater*. He also became a good friend, but it took a while.

Things were moving along well until the end of the second year when we were told that the following year there would no longer be a junior high school in our county. Ninth graders would return to high schools, as freshmen (where they had started originally). That meant, middle school was coming in with grades 6th, 7th and 8th, but not for me. I told the principal I was not interested in teaching younger students and asked for a transfer to high school.

I was offered the three schools closest to where I lived: luckily for me, all three were in need of a theater teacher. For me, the decision was an easy one. Two of the three schools were in no way air conditioned; the third was. I was more than ready to enjoy the experience of teaching in a real, air conditioned school, especially one that had an auditorium, complete with stage, balcony, and lights. And so I went to Loch Raven High School. I thought I had died and gone to heaven.

CHAPTER TWENTY-EIGHT:

INTO THE 80'S

The late 70's and early 80's were a very busy time for Doris, but not in the world of entertainment. In 1976, she married Barry Comden, a marriage that lasted five years. In late 1979, he convinced her to buy a large complex and settle in the hills of Carmel, California, a place she had fallen in love with while filming *Julie*. Her beautiful home and complex overlooks one of the local golf courses. Golfers say they often see Doris on her balcony, and of course she waves to them. (On occasion, she even yells out a comment or two).

Not too long after settling in Carmel, Barry was gone, and Doris lived on the hill with her animals. About that, she has said: "I never could pick a husband". As for Barry, he felt she loved the dogs more than him. I guess the best response to that one is: no comment.

The busiest part of her life was (and still is) animal advocacy and animal welfare, and no one does it better. She was all over the place, fighting the cause for animals and dodging paparazzi who kept trying to make her a Greta Garbo-like recluse. One article in *The Globe* disturbed me so much that I just had to write and be assured that everything was all right. It must have also disturbed a lot of other fans because a form letter was forthcoming with the correct assurance for all her fans. On it, Doris had penned a short note to me: "I am fine, Mike…not to worry. Everything is just great. You can't believe anything you read in those rag papers." Usually, Doris ignored all those insulting articles in *The Globe* or *The Enquirer* but one time she sued them and quickly got a printed retraction in the paper, which is all she wanted anyway. Doris has always said that instead of buying those gossip papers, we should send that money to her animal foundation, where it would get much better use. She's right! My comment is this: if Doris is a recluse and long forgotten, as the paper so often implies, then why does her picture appear on the front pages as often as it does? The answer, even

at 88, and long out of the public eye, Doris
still sells papers, as she always did!

At one point in the 80's , Terry convinced
his mother to buy into the Cypress Inn, a bed
and breakfast hotel in the heart of Carmel, as
a proprietor and co-owner. Today, that hotel
has become one of the most pet-friendly
hotels in the United States, and Doris is
always pleased to get letters from satisfied
patrons, both two and four leggers! Visitors
there can see signs of Doris everywhere
(wall posters, furnishings, animals in
abundance, Terry's Lounge, etc.) The only
thing they don't see is Doris. When I was
there in February, 2012, the staff of the hotel
said, sadly, that they had not seen her in
person in years. That is today, but in the
80's, Doris was not in hiding.

In 1985, Terry and the Christian Broadcast
Cable Network talked Doris into another TV
series, which only lasted a year. It was
called *Doris Day's Best Friends*. Of course,
the attraction for Doris was two-fold. First
and foremost, it gave her a great opportunity
to continue her pleas for animal welfare.
Each show highlighted some aspect of
animal welfare, usually with a local vet in
place. Also, this show gave Doris the
opportunity to invite some of her Hollywood

friends for some heartfelt reminiscences. It was her first time back on TV since the mid 70's when she appeared on various talk shows to publicize the book she co-wrote with A.E. Hotchner, *Her Own Story*, (a Top Ten Seller on the *New York Times* book list.)

When the show was about to launch, the publicity was bigger than anyone could have ever imagined. She had invited longtime friend, Rock Hudson, to be her first guest and to join her to publicize the show. When he showed up, everyone was in for a shock. Rock had developed some kind of rare disease at the time (which was diagnosed as AIDS). He did not look well at all. Doris wanted him to remain at her home so she could nurse him back to health, but that was not to be. As he had promised her, he came to Carmel to film one of the show's first episodes. Once that promise was completed, Rock flew to Paris to a clinic specializing in the treatment of this rare disease, to no avail. He died there.

What was supposed to be the first episode of the show was held back because of Hudson's death, and that episode of the show (which aired after Rock's death) became one of the most popular broadcasts of the year. It was very poignant, especially the eulogy Doris gave to Rock and the song she chose in honor of him, "My Buddy" (which recently became the same song she chose to honor the memory of her son.) This episode of the show can be seen on YouTube; however, the full series of the show has still not been released for purchase. No one seems to know why.

It was a very interesting show for many reasons. First, it brought Doris back into the public eye, just as bright and happy and healthy as always. And viewers could certainly enjoy the beautiful scenery in and around Carmel by The Sea, California. Doris had many famous guests besides Rock, including Angie Dickinson, Les Brown and his Band, Tony Randall, Howard Keel, Robert Wagner, Tony Bennett, and Cleveland Amory. It also gave Doris (spurred on by Terry) an opportunity to sing again and most shows sported at least one song sung by her. Those songs, never released, recently became the nucleus of the album in 2011/2012 , *My Heart*, which became a top ten international best seller.

Also, in 1985, Doris appeared in a British produced television special called *I Don't Even Like Apple Pie*. In the show's interview with Doris, she debunked her image of The All American Girl, thus the show's title. A write up of the show was part of one of TV Guide's weekly issues, but the show itself was never released on American television. How typical.

In 1989, Doris surfaced once again. It was the final time that she appeared at a public gathering. This time, she was to be the recipient of The Cecil B. DeMille Award for Lifetime Achievement in Acting, presented by the Golden Globes, an honor long overdue. On their behalf, I commend them for the many Golden Globes bestowed on Doris through the years. This group got it right!

The ceremony was in Los Angeles. No one is certain how he did it, but Terry convinced Doris to go, and he went with her. The award was presented by her California neighbor, and former Mayor of Carmel, Clint Eastwood. Her acceptance speech is one of the better ones ever presented in this kind of situation. That, too, is available on YouTube. Doris got two standing ovations.

That award and TV appearance was perfect timing for Doris, alive and well in the 80's. She looked wonderful, she spoke eloquently and even flirted with Host Clint Eastwood (both indicated they would like to have done a picture together). The highlight of her speech was the portion where she said she'd been away too long and needed to come back. Everyone agreed. But as we all know, it never happened.

As for me, I was enjoying some of the best years of my life in teaching. I found the high school ages of the students delightful. We could talk on a mature basis (yes, 9th graders, too). We could treat each other with mutual respect and get on with the daily business of learning…me, too. I taught students in the Gifted and Talented group and Honor Student group. I was constantly challenged to do more and more to inspire those students to reach their academic heights. With Chaucer, Shakespeare and Dickens as part of the program, my degrees in English Literature were being put to constant use. Students who thought they would hate Shakespearean plays wanted to do more and more and more. We covered everything from *Hamlet* to *King Lear*. They enjoyed the challenge of acting it out, especially when they realized that the words of the Master were indeed anything but gobbledygook.

My department chairman and administrative staff were very supportive of me, not only in the area of teaching, but also in the theater arts department. I started with my first Theater I class, which met in the auditorium instead of a classroom (pretty fitting, I would say). We started by sitting on the stage in a circle of friends, and that is exactly what we became. This program became very popular, and the scheduling administrator thought he could just dump anyone into the course for an easy "A". He and the students learned very quickly that was not the case, but they stayed, and some actually got A's, but it was anything but easy. They started with theater exercises and improvisation and eventually wound up by doing full scenes from famous plays, each complete with costumes, staging and learned lines as an exam.

Since the class was open only to 10th, 11th and 12th graders as an elective, 9th grade students began pressuring the guidance office for their inclusion. By the second year, I had two Theater I classes and one Theater II class. Instead of 3 periods a week for ½ a credit, we met 5 periods a week for ¾ a credit. The creative office staff found a way to include 9th graders at least 2 days a week. On the two periods when they were not in gym, they had 2 study periods. They could schedule those periods with me as Drama Aides for no credit. One year, I had 11 Aides.

Eventually, we got permission for those students who wished to do a semi-major in theater, to get Theater II, which met as a separate class. Then Theater Arts III and IV were included in elective offerings. These students were assigned with the Theater I or Theater II classes and could serve in some capacities as student teachers. This became very important when we got to some of the special skill areas in which I was not much of an expert, such as mime.

This cadre of students also formed the nucleus of a performing company, and we would entertain various elementary, middle schools and senior centers on a fairly often basis. They were also allowed to meet with the Theater II classes if their schedule could accommodate it. Each year, this group would put on an entertaining assembly for the school, featuring all kinds of varied performance. Some years, we did two assemblies and these were always popular functions.

The advanced theater class also had as a major activity a full-fledged play performance for a weekend which was not open casting. We would select a show and then mount it, to use a theatrical term. The students were responsible for the entire thing, and I do not mean one-act plays. We cast it. We staged it. We costumed it. We got stage and lighting crews. And we even had student directors usually those with the most experience. One year, we did *Our Town* and another year we did *If A Man Answers*. These productions were always done in February when very little else was happening at school. As a result, the weekend performances were well attended.

In some cases, I saw some of the same students in a theater capacity three periods a day! Since I had many of them in one of my English classes, that meant I saw some of them even four times a day. Then, many of them were also involved with the actual performing aspect of the drama program, so I also saw them in the evening. We did indeed become a family. They became very important to me, especially on such family occasions as the deaths of my father and mother (9 years apart). Many of them were there for the funeral services. I still see some of them today, and we have also become friends on Facebook.

The drama class, however, had nothing to do with the Theater Arts Performing Program, which was done totally outside of class in the evening. We called ourselves The Loch Raven Stage Company, and I am happy to say we had a reputation among other schools in the county as one of the better performing groups. I always tried to instill in the kids the philosophy that I learned from Doris... like it or hate it, give it 100 percent and do the best you can do every time.

We produced two major shows a year. In the fall, we usually did a comedy or drama. In the spring, we did a full-fledged musical in conjunction with the Music and often the Art Department. This was a real challenge because the stage (with no curtain) was built to house the Baltimore Symphony until they got their new home at the Meyerhoff in downtown Baltimore. In the first few years, that alone created problems because if we had sets on the stage when the symphony was performing on a weekend, they had to be disassembled and moved. We also had to schedule rehearsals and performances around their schedule. It was a blessing when they finally moved out, but then, a local church moved in for Sunday morning worship services while their church was being built. That, too, became a headache but they at least worked with our sets!

Getting used to a stage which seemed like a mile from side to side was not an easy adjustment. There were no spaces above from which to fly scenery so everything had to be portable. Eventually, but it took a year, we learned to adapt to the stage. The first year, the first play, was the most difficult. We produced a thriller, *The Bad Seed*, and we packed the house. For the Spring musical that year, we chose *Annie Get Your Gun*. We thought it would be simple, it wasn't. Fireworks and horse riding without horses became a challenge. The actors were up to the challenge, they gave it their best, and we had another good house.

But a packed house like I have never seen before came the following spring when we did *South Pacific*. Publicity became a big thing: we learned quickly how important it is to publicize well. Leis (a prominent costume accessory in the play) became a big part of the campaign. Just use your vivid imagination. We even performed a "preview" show for the entire school (a 20 minute teaser, performed twice, once for

9/10 grade and once for 11/12 grade.) We found a friend in the community who was a talented artist who volunteered to help with scenery. He discovered that our auditorium stage had a rear projection wall. Before long, we had Bali Hai in the background, complete with waves rolling in from the sea to the shore line, where various palm trees and sand had been placed all over the stage to represent the South Pacific.

In addition, when the school auditorium was built, they had put in two little balconies above and to the left and right of the stage. These became the setting for those scenes that did not need the full stage. It was a trip for the actors to run from the main stage, up the back stairs and out on balcony one or two for their next scene, and then back to the main stage. All in a night's fun!

Tickets were sold in advance with $1 off if purchased then. The first night of the show, we only had 120 tickets left to sell at the door. They were gone within 15 minutes of opening the doors. We had to turn away 85 people that night because the auditorium (and the balcony) were completely sold out! We also set up a ticket book in the lobby after the show for tickets for the following night. (As was my usual case, I had double cast the leads in the show to bring in crowds both nights). Many people wanted to see both performances. After the first show, we sold all our remaining tickets for the second night. On that second night, we had to post signs on the door that the performance was sold out! I can't tell you how happy that made everyone involved.

A little footnote to that experience. I had all the adults who helped with the show (musical director, orchestra conductor, props, costumes and make-up chairmen, refreshment coordinator, etc.) over to my house after the show for drinks and food. We had been assembled for less than an hour when we heard this racket on the front lawn. Lo and behold, it was the entire cast of the show (all 75 of them) on my front lawn in a long line singing "There is Nothing Like A Dame" still in costume and make-up. They serenaded the entire neighborhood. Trust me, there was nothing like it! Yes, when I told her about this, Doris thought it was such a "kick", to use her term.

Some of the shows after *South Pacific* which were among our most successful were: *The Miracle Worker, Auntie Mame, Hello Dolly!, Barefoot in the Park, Guys and*

Dolls, Fiddler on the Roof and *Arsenic and Old Lace*. No matter what the show, during those years we always had a really large attendance, but nothing ever packed the house again like *South Pacific*. By the way, the staircase we built for *Mame* which we also used for *Dolly* got us into trouble with the fire department, but we used it anyway.

From 1981 to 1990, I continued to teach theater classes and do three shows a year for weekend performances. Added to that was my usual teaching schedule from 6:30 a.m. till 3 p.m. daily, followed by evening rehearsals from 5:30 till 11 two days a week. Add to that the required lesson planning, grading papers, attending meetings, chaperone duties and all the other things required of a busy English/Theater teacher and you will understand why the usual correspondence between Doris and me those years was nothing if not spotty. Spotty, yes...but it never completely stopped.

One such note to Doris from me occurred in one of my last years of teaching theater. We were doing some routine exercises in a Theater II class. I told one of the female actors to give the scene a typical Doris Day reaction. I got a blank look. And then she said, "Who is Doris Day?" As I look back at it now, I guess it would have been funny to an onlooker, because if there were 35 students in the class, I am relatively certain that at least 30 of them not only knew who she was but also knew of my passion for her. So…30 pairs of eyes first looked at me, then looked back at the young lady who had made such a grave error. I took it in stride, told the entire class to form a friendship circle. I then proceeded to give them a research and oral performance assignment (this, remember, on the spur of the moment). From the top of my pointed head, I started to gather a list of names. I told them to raise their hand as I said a name if they had never heard of the person. The names that I can recall now included: Spencer Tracey, June Allyson, Michael Curtis, Ethel Barrymore, Van Johnson, Bob Fosse, Carol Haney, Richard Rogers, Lorenz Hart, and many others of the same ilk. Their assignment was to research and prepare an informational audio visual performance project in which they told the other members of the class about the importance of this person to the entertainment industry. They were told the presentation could be no less than 20 minutes and no more than 40 minutes (a class period was usually 50 minutes). The young lady who had asked the question and precipitated my response was given Doris

Day as her topic. I gave them two weeks and made sure I had VCRs, TVs and movie projectors available for all those periods when presentations were scheduled.

It turned out to be the best assignment I ever gave to an Advanced Theater Class. They really got into it and thoroughly enjoyed it. I still get comments today about how much they liked that assignment. And trust me, the performances were truly marvelous, but none was as remarkable as the young lady who had Doris as her topic.

Briefly, she started by turning on a cassette player, on which she had recorded a medley of Doris' most popular songs, which she ran in the background of her talk for a full 40 minutes. She then turned on the TV and put in a home recorded tape on which she had excerpts from at least 25 of Doris' 39 movies. That excerpt lasted for about 15 minutes. She followed that with the usual bio information done in a question/answer format (she played two parts: the interviewer and the interviewee, a Doris expert). The questions covered most aspects of Doris career, like: "Did Doris always want to be an actress" to "Why did she retire from show business". Her talk ended by stating that she believed Doris Day should have an academy award for some of her movies. And then she showed excerpts (again on tape) of: *Love Me or Leave Me, Pillow Talk, Midnight Lace,* and a scene from *The Man Who Knew Too Much.* When she was finished the entire class was smiling. They looked at me and I was smiling, too. Everyone knew they had just seen an A+ performance and that young lady will never ask that question again! Doris thought this incident was really great. She loved hearing about it. And she thought the assignment I gave was a pertinent one to the situation. As I said, they all enjoyed doing it and listening to it as well.

I stopped directing plays and teaching theater a couple years before I retired from teaching. It was pretty much the same thing and yet different. In the theater program, the kids were not as willing to learn lines, to really put forth the effort. Oh sure, they wanted to "shine" on the stage, but not because they were good…rather because they were who they were. You can well imagine how I responded to that attitude. To give less than 100 percent went against everything I believed in. So, I told my department chairman and principal to find someone else and let me concentrate on teaching English, my first love.

And that I did. But then, something happened there as well. We were being asked to "teach to tests". It was important that a student be able to respond well on test questions and do well on the tests given by the county each year. Test achievement is only one part of what makes a good student. There was no longer any place for creativity. Once creativity is stifled, for me, there is not much left. So, when the opportunity arose in 1991, I retired from teaching. Yes, I still miss it, but I hear it is still not a very creative endeavor. Perhaps I should spell it out. What I do miss is the students---the special relationships we had. I miss the actual job of teaching because I loved helping the students find delight in literature (very few ever found delight in grammar or spelling). I certainly do not miss the on-site things: faculty meetings and any other kind of meeting of which there are far too many in any given month, grading papers (I would much rather have one on one conferences), doing report cards (a necessary evil) and all the ungodly paper work associated with the job. I might have gone on to something like a college subject (poetry, Shakespeare, whatever), but at the time I retired, I really believed 33 years was quite enough. It was time to do something else.

I went back the next year for one half a year to fill in for a teacher who was having a serious operation. I started the year with a group of 10th and 11th grade students, and I loved them. They liked me, too, which was cool. But then Christmas came, and it was time for their "assigned" teacher to return. None of us were happy, but it was what it was. I still hear to this day from many of those students who wished I could have stayed all year. Honestly, I felt the same way. Substituting for someone else is never as good as the real thing.

And so I decided that if it was not my very own class, there was no use doing it. I settled into retirement for good at about the same time that computers were starting to make an important mark on the world. And so, both Doris and I moved on into the 90's. I bought a computer and learned how to use it; I think Doris is just now enjoying an iPod or an iPad.

.

CHAPTER TWENTY-NINE :

THE NINETIES AND BEYOND

Doris continued to be, and is still, very active with animal welfare. When she appeared in public after 1990, it was almost exclusively to further her cause for the animals. She sat for occasional interviews with various people throughout the 90's:

- ♥ a show called "Sentimental Journey" in 1991 for PBS
- ♥ an interview with Gloria Hunniford for the BBC in 1994
- ♥ an interview with Des O'Connor on the release of the long lost album alternately called *The Lost Album* or *The Love Album* released in the UK in 1994 but not in the US until 2006.

To say that the US is way behind the UK in anything Doris Day is definitely a complete understatement. This was the last time that she appeared anywhere on public TV live.

All future interviews, and there have been many in the last few years, were via phone with the interviewer. These included a 1998 biography called *It's Magic* for A&E, a 2002 BBC special called *Hollywood Greats: Doris Day,* an *E! True Hollywood Story* in 2002 and a special German documentary produced by ARTE in 2009 called *What a Difference a DAY Made.*

There has been a dramatic surge of Doris popularity once again in the last few years, beginning with the publication of various books about Doris, her life and her career. Among the better ones, and ones that Doris liked, were: *Considering Doris Day* by Tom Santopietro, *Doris Day* by Eric Braun and *The Doris Day Companion: A Beautiful Day* by Pierre Patrick. There were others not favored by the star, who informed fans via internet: "Rather than spend your money on these books, send a donation to my pet foundation. Read my own biography if you want to know the details of my life." These included a rather sensationalized memoir from one of her former personal assistants who was fired for being far and away too meddlesome. The book is extremely bold especially in the narrative of things that were never meant to see the light of day and much too personal for any reader. The others that did not sit well with Doris were books that had exactly the same cover, only the titles were different. These were written by two men, both named David. Since her own biography was such an open and honest telling of her story, that should be the one first selected.

From 2008 on, numerous interviews, articles, birthday celebrations and phone calls are very much a part of keeping Doris in the public eye, especially with the release of her three new CDs: *My Heart*, *With a Smile and a Song* and *The Ultimate Collection*, proceeds from which help support the Doris Day Animal Foundation. She tells me that her fan mail today is just as exhaustive as it was at the peak of her popularity in the 1950's and 1960's and a constant source of worry for her, too. She has always personally responded in some way to all of her fan mail, but now it is hard for her to keep up with it, and she seeks the help from friends and staff as well. She continues to take an active part in each response if only to sign her name and underline various comments. On my online website, www.sampod4u.com, you can hear her talk about this issue and thank her many friends for their continued interest in her and her career.

Retirement for me has been rewarding and extremely busy. I sometimes wonder how I ever had time to teach. I have to say the world of the internet has kept me extremely busy and my mind very active (not a bad thing). I once said I would read all the books on my bookshelf when I retired, but they still sit there. Most of the reading I do is internet reading, even if it is a book. Those I read when I download them on my Nook or Kindle, along with the fun and popular games like Angry Birds which intrigue me. I have become a fairly good player of Gin Rummy and Dominos and enjoy occasional Internet Bridge as well. But my time is also shared with travel, friends, animals, my website, my music and, most of all, lots of Doris.

I recently discovered Sirius XM Radio and their various music channels. They even have dedicated stations to stars like Frank Sinatra and Elvis, but not to Doris. I keep writing them and complaining about that. If Pandora can have not one but three Doris Day Stations, Sirius XM could have at least one. I give them credit for playing a Doris record once in a while (on 40's or 50's featured stations and even on Siriusly Sinatra), but it is too few and far between. Sinatra, admittedly, was a big star and sold lots of records, but so did Doris. Other stars, too, deserve dedicated stations, like: Perry Como, Teresa Brewer, Jo Stafford and Eddie Fisher. Come on, Sirius, get serious!

My constant internet search for Doris led me to a fun activity which took much of my time in 2010. I found this station out of Virginia which not only played Doris, but they played her a lot. So, I called the station and told them how much I enjoyed their music and to keep up the good work. That phone call led the station owner to ask me to sponsor a show dedicated to Doris. I accepted graciously and, for the first time in my life, I took on a job I had always wanted to try: that of being a disc jockey and show moderator/producer. We called the show *A Sentimental Journey with Doris Day and Her Friends*, which allowed me to bring in records by others who also ruled the airwaves in the 1950's like Doris did. But mostly, it was a full career retrospective of all her recorded (and non-recorded) music as well.

We broadcast every Sunday at 3 p.m. and eventually the broadcasts were expanded to several days, nights and early mornings throughout the week. I began with the first year in which Doris started singing, her audition for Barney Rapp, and continued to tell the musical story of her life, pretty much from 1939 through her last few recordings in 1986 (the ones which became the nucleus for her album, *My Heart)*. We hosted a three hour birthday broadcast that year and had thousands of listeners as we streamed live over the internet. I also ended up doing a series of special programs titled "Just For Old Time's Sake" broadcast on other different days. Some of these programs can still be viewed on www.youtube.com. If you have a computer, you can still hear a couple of for instances:

http://www.youtube.com/watch?v=Z6vQmp
EmZxA
http://www.youtube.com/watch?v=YHac5w
BN454
http://www.youtube.com/watch?v=hfNneD
HUEP8

That was a very enjoyable experience for me that year. I not only had the chance to play Doris music for what amounted to 24 installments covering her full recording career, but we did special programs on her *Songs of Faith, Songs of Christmas, Her Top 100 Hit Parade Songs, Her Broadway Songs* on another show we called *The Doris Day Songbook.*

It took a vast amount of my time to write the scripts, select the music and air the shows, but it was great fun doing what I like to do best: share my love for Doris and her work. And when it expanded to being able to share other great artists as well, I was in 7th heaven. But towards the end of that year, in December, the station owner and I had a major falling out. We just didn't agree on the direction in which the programming format was heading, and so we parted company. I certainly owe a large debt of gratitude to him because he taught me a lot of technical skills about working on the internet with music, as well as how to edit and recombine music files. I learned a bit about how to publicize a show as well, and had fun doing "teasers" for the radio.

For two months, there was no activity, but activity was definitely in the works. This time, one of my favorite people and a close friend, Sue Schoeffield, was busily putting together a website where I could continue to indulge in and share my Doris Day music.

We launched SAMPOD4U.COM in February. At the time, our format was shared music in podcast format. The viewer and listener simply clicked on the audio themed files, which lasted anywhere from 30 minutes to an hour or so each. Sue and I each had several themed shows that we produced, and the website launched new shows about every 3 weeks.

But once we found that it was going to be too expensive to continue paying copyright fees to play the music, we changed the format to links where the music could be heard. That was the first year, and we had a good time working together on producing a fun website. We even brought in a few of our friends as guest artists. Susan eventually got interested in doing other things, and so she went on to a few of her own websites, but has graciously stayed hooked up with sampod, especially whenever we needed help with things technical, never my forte.

When www.spotify.com came into prominence, we were once again able to do podcasts with links to playlists on Spotify which are completely legal and license paid. That and YouTube are the sources of the music we provide today (starting our 3rd year in February 2013), and we do movies and TV as well. The site is growing in popularity each day, especially our Forum and the "Just Doris Day" pages, our most popular.

In each of the two years of operation, we have received and posted audio messages from Doris herself thanking us for playing so much of her music. In addition, Doris has posted, on her own website, a link to ours. That was a huge day in my life, but there were two others. One was the phone call in March 2012, which you have already read about. (For the other, see the Afterward section.)

My radio experience also gave me the opportunity to meet and befriend Carol Johnson in Georgia, our forum moderator. Carol has been to visit Doris in person in California twice, and I keep telling her that soon, we are going to go together and take Doris to dinner. (We can dream...) We share a love for Doris and enjoy working together and chatting almost every day either by phone or on the internet. We have visited twice in Baltimore, and now she says it is my turn to trek to Atlanta. Because of the forum, we have had the opportunity to also befriend Christie Sietos (a wonderful Greek girl schooling in Canterbury, UK) and

305

Janet Moore (a delightful young lady in Boston, Massachusetts). Christie and Janet have become the nucleus of our tech staff on the website, and we are very happy to have them. We have a cadre of regular forum talkers, and we call them "the sampod family"…what we share in common is a profound affection for Doris Day.

Do I miss the radio show? Yes, I do. Would I do it again? Probably in a heartbeat. The director of the station has called/written to me several times since and asked if I would like to try again. I was not able to say "yes" because I have been so busy with sampod. If asked again, I might change my mind. I do miss the "radio format" and the "live broadcasts". Why would I change my mind? Because sampod is in pretty good working order at the moment (when our provider, Weebly, is not messing up), and I could probably find the time to do another Doris Day Radio Program. She is so popular right now, the show would be, too.

My correspondence with Doris in the past few years has become more like a close friendship. She does not refer to me as a fan but as a friend. And we are on a first name basis. I really love that. In our letters, we converse as friends, and so I feel like I have become part of her family, and I love the fact that she considers me her friend. She has made my life a constant joy, and she has certainly been one of the most consistent things in my life, all my life.

AFTERWARD

There have been several constants in my
life, but the most consistent and long-lasting
one has been this wonderful albeit distant
relationship I have had with Doris. It has
comforted and sustained me all these years,
and if I never meet her in person, I am
secure in my belief that she will be in
Heaven, and I will meet her there. (No, I
have never considered the alternative.)

Another constant is my love of music, which
I was aware of as a small child in the crib. I
have records, CDs, tapes all over the house,
and they invade all but the bathrooms
(where I have portable radios to listen to
music there), and they dominate three
computers and other electronic modes. My
tastes are very eclectic (more so than you
can possibly imagine), and they include all
phases of music with just a very few
exceptions. I never liked rap or hip hop. I
consider that nothing more than syncopated
rhythm. As a poetry teacher for many years,

if my students would read a poem aloud in that sing song rhythm, I would not be a happy camper; it destroys the meaning. That said, another exception would be improve or progressive jazz. I did not rule out jazz, only jazz with no melody. I have never been a fan of improvisation…not on the stage, not in comedy routines, and certainly not in music. And the other form of music not in my collection is what I would call pure hillbilly music (you know, Hank Snow, Hank Williams, their predecessors or followers). I'll take my country music without the twang, thank you. On the other hand, I have some recordings I prize by Lefty Frizzell, Red Foley (with the Andrews Sisters) and Ferlin Husky…so I didn't rule all of that out. No apology here to my sister, Roseanne, who is a hillbilly through and through, at least in her musical tastes.

Still one more constant in my life has been my best friend, my partner, my housemate, Chris. We have shared a life since 1970, and I honestly cannot see my life without him. He has been a source of affection for many years, and I am happy he shares his life with me. He is not particularly a Doris fanatic like me. He enjoys her work and tolerates my obsession. He was just as happy when I got the phone call from her as I was.

That said, the original Doris/Les version of *Sentimental Journey* is one of his favorite records; he says so every time he hears it.

But when all is said and done, the largest constant in my life has been this thing with Doris. It is hard to define, but I wouldn't change it for anything. Maybe "affair" was the wrong choice of a title, I am not sure. However, one definition of the word is "a lively enthusiasm"…certainly this has been a truism. And I thank Doris for sharing my life with me: because of her I have been a better person. Because of her I understand giving 100 percent.

In April of 2012, I was totally shocked by an early surprise party for my 75th Birthday. It was sponsored by my partner, Chris Pawlowski, who invited a number of our friends to share my birthday and have dinner on him. It was a wonderful gathering attended by 25 or so of our favorite people. After several hours of conversation and dinner, I opened the gifts. When I thought I had finished, my friend Carol from Georgia said, "I have one more". Whereupon, she opened and read the following letter:

Dear Mike:

HAPPY 75TH BIRTHDAY!

I know you are enjoying your wonderful "surprise" party with all of your family and friends. I'm pleased that you consider me one of your friends, as well.

Now, I want you to know how much I appreciate your support through your website, Mike, and your thoughtful gifts to the four-leggers-it really means a lot to me.

So, stay well my friend, and have fun at your party!

With my love,

Doris "and my babies"

This is a photo of the Birthday Letter from Doris:

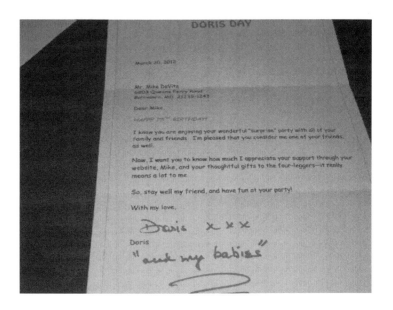

It took 75 years, but what a great birthday present! And I think a fitting ending to my story.

POST SCRIPTS:

I have said very little in the past few pages about my family. As I indicated earlier, I only brought them in to the story as enablers, as background to the total picture. However, that said, you should know that as I turned 75, I have no one of my previously mentioned family members left in my native town of Allentown. Mom died at the ripe old age of 101; Grammy died at 102. Pop died at 65 (young, I think…). My father died in 1981; mother died in 1991, the year I became an orphan of sorts. All of my aunts and uncles with whom I grew up...Anna, Buddy, Helen...all gone, some of them for over 20 years. I miss them still. After all, they are the ones who started me on my lifelong quest for Doris or supported that quest by never being unsympathetic. I have been lucky that way all my life. My sisters (all three of them) and my brothers (both of them), my partner and all my friends have always been supportive as well. I thank them all for their tolerance and love.

I have had thousands of students over the 33 plus years in which I taught (everything from English, to journalism, to Speech and Theater Arts). All of them were special: I never had a student I didn't like, and I realize that is not the usual case. I guess I was just lucky. Some stand out more than others for various reasons. But in all those years, I can definitely single out someone who was very special to me. He was bright, he was enthusiastic, he was caring, he was thoughtful, he was challenging, he was talented, he was the son I never had but wanted...all those things teachers wish for in a student and in a lifelong friend. His name is Dan Funk. We first met when I began my four years at Cockeysville High School in 1967. I started during the summer, and he was one of the first to stop that summer to say hello and meet the person who would be his English teacher. I met him and his parents, who had just moved from Massachusetts to Maryland. We all hit it off immediately, and I found that they lived across the street from me in Briarcliff Apartments. That was the beginning of a lifelong friendship I value to this day.

Dan was invited to my 75th surprise party and could not come. Here is the letter he sent, and I am pretty sure he will not mind my sharing:

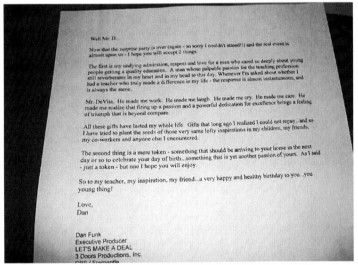

If there is a problem reading the text of the letter, it is shown next:

" Well Mr. D...

*Now that the surprise party is over (again-
so sorry I couldn't attend!!) and the real
event is almost upon us – I hope you will
accept two things.*

*The first is my undying admiration, respect
and love for a man who cared so deeply
about young people getting a quality
education. A man whose palpable passion
for the teaching profession still reverberates
in my heart and in my head to this day.
Whenever I'm asked about whether I had a
teacher who truly made a difference in my
life – the response is almost instantaneous,
and it is always the same.*

*Mr. DeVita. He made me work. He made
me laugh. He made me cry. He made me
care. He made me realize that firing up a
passion and a powerful dedication for
excellence brings a feeling of triumph that is
beyond compare.*

*All these gifts have lasted my whole life.
Gifts that long ago I realized I could not
repay...and so I have tried to plant the seeds
of those very same lofty inspirations in my*

children, my friends, my co-workers and anyone else I encountered.

The second thing is a mere token – something that should be arriving to your home in the next day or so to celebrate the day of your birth...something that is yet another passion of yours. As I said – just a token – but one I hope you will enjoy.

So to my teacher, my inspiration, my friend...a very happy and healthy birthday to you...you young thing!

Love,
Dan"

Dan Funk
Executive Producer
LET'S MAKE A DEAL
3 Doors Productions, Inc.
CBS/Fremantle

Here is the "mere token" he sent as a gift:

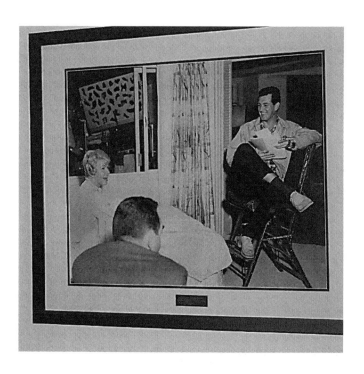

Of course the picture is of Doris with Rock Hudson and the film's director in an informal moment on the set of *Pillow Talk* in 1959.

Here was my response to that gift, and his response back:

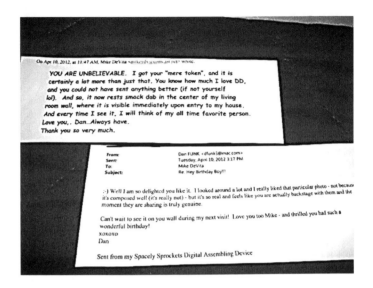

Text of my email to Dan reads:

"YOU ARE UNBELIEVABLE. I got your "mere token", and it is certainly a lot more than just that. You know how much I love DD, and you could not have sent anything better (if not yourself lol). And so, it now rests smack dab in the center of my living room wall, where it is visible immediately upon entry to my house. And every time I see it, I will think of my all time favorite person.
Love you, Dan…Always have.
Thanks you so very much."

And here is the text of his response email:

318

*" ☺ Well I am so delighted you like it. I
looked around a lot and I really liked that
particular photo – not because it's
composed well (it's really not) – but it's so
real and feels like you are actually
backstage with them and the moment they
are sharing is truly genuine.*

*Can't wait to see it on your wall during my
next visit! Love you too Mike – and thrilled
you had such a wonderful birthday!*
xoxoxo
Dan"

And there you have it. Anyone who knows
me well knows my passion. All my family
always knew it. All my close students knew
it. All my close friends knew it. Dan knew
it. Doris knows it, too! And now, so do you.